CHUCKING GRANNY

A HUNDRED LIVES THROUGH THE EYES OF AN EMT

Dedication

To Slate, my constant inspiration and muse

To I and W, for keeping me sane in an insane time

TABLE OF CONTENTS

27 and 28. The Lucy Truck

29. The Player

30. The Ditz

31. The Quiet Racist

32. The Night Shift Queen

33. The Cursed Ginger

34. The Overly Dramatic One

35. The Drag Strip Queen

36. The Man On His Way Out

37. The Crush

38. The Father Figure

39. The Whipped Boyfriend

40. The Squirrel

41 and 42. The Twins

43. The Dwarf

44. The Contradiction

45. The Creep

46. The Pre-Divorcee

47. The Medic Tamer

48. The Artsy Chick

49. The Younger Brother

50 and 51. The Special Ones

52. The Semi-Regular Partner

53. The Absent Minded Professor

54. The Closeted Gay One

55. The New Yorker

56. The Perfect Newbie

57. The Government Conspiracist

58. A Girl

59. The Lesbian

60. The Constant Complainer

61. The Secret Badass

62. The Immortal One

63. The Conservative

64. The Redneck Dipper

65 and 66. The Husband and Wife Team

67. The Passive Aggressive Bitch

68. The Gentle Giant

69. The Soccer Mom

70. The Nameless

71. The Self Assured Fireman

72. The Humble Firefighter

73. The Mini-Me

74. The Overshare

75. The Worst Day

76. The New Person

77. The Unlucky One

78. The Unapologetic Douche-nozzle

79. The Other Company Man

80. The Smoker

81. The Soulmate

82. My First Medic

83. The Boyfriend

84. The Asshole

Preface - Proper PPE

Bit of an introduction. I am an Emergency Medical Technician or EMT. For those of you not familiar, that is the person who goes around transports sick and injured folk to the hospital in an ambulance. In EMS, emergency medical services, we use a lot of abbreviations, like PPE, personal protective equipment. We always make sure to don our gloves and any other protective gear before we make patient contact. So in order to fully understand this story I need to give you all a little background.

When I first started working on this monstrosity I had no idea that I would actually get this far. I started writing this novella because I hated the company I worked for and needed a way to blow off steam. However this soon took shape into the thing you see today.

In each of the following chapters I describe an EMS partner I have had in my two years of working at a backup 911 transfer EMS service named Ryder EMS (not its real name of course - I mean I still have to work there).

In the city I work in, I'll call it The City (because I am extremely imaginative), there is one 911 EMS service and the rest are transfer companies like Ryder. At Ryder we mostly do transfers (hospital to hospital, hospital to nursing home, hospital to home, anywhere to dialysis) and we provide backup 911 service to The City. However once you get outside The City we are the only ambulance service and provide 911 coverage to those areas.

As a mostly transfer service my EMS experience was a bit different than your "normal" EMT. In the two years I have worked as an EMT for Ryder I can number my true blue, blood and gore experiences on one hand. This story is not one of riveting tales of crazy patients and the psychological toll of dealing with death on a daily basis.

This book is titled, <u>Chucking Granny</u>, because that is what we do at transfer services. We move Granny from one place to the next and ensure that she doesn't suddenly stop living from point A to point B. We call it "chucking" because those absorbent pads we sometimes place under our patients to catch certain bodily fluids are called "chucks". Yep, at Ryder and other transfer services we are just a bunch of Motherchuckers.

My story is about the people I got to know in perhaps one of the most intimate settings there is: confined to a metal box on wheels for anywhere from twelve to twenty four hours at a time.

It is absolutely astounding what you can learn from people when you're forced to take care of patients together in a high stress job. You lend your partner your temporary trust. You trust them to do their jobs (if not well). You sort of have to give them this trust, because there is no one else. It is just you and him or her against the grannies of the world. (Hey there are some fierce grannies out there.)

What follows is an honest, or an as honest as I can manage, account of each of these EMTs and Paramedics. For obvious reasons all names are changed, and due to the pseudo-military atmosphere of EMS all involved are referred to by their fake last names, except for me. You can call me:

E.S.T.

1 and 2. The Introduction to Ryder EMS, Part One

I am a semi intelligent individual. I graduated with a bachelor's in biochemistry from an excellent hole in the wall college and did enough grad school to know I hated research. So I dropped out and instantly became one of those directionless twenty somethings. I was over educated and unemployed and applying to fast food joints.

Then a friend suggested I become an EMT. I wanted to end up in the medical field, so I thought it was the perfect short term option. That's how I found myself in Ryder EMS's accelerated EMT course. Eight weeks and I'd be done. The class itself gave me no trouble and I found myself forced to hold my tongue in deference to my classmates. It was difficult, but I kept my arrogance to low levels.

Along with the class we had to clock in twenty four hours of "Ride Time" where we ride along on the ambulance. Twenty four hours of playing the game of sit down, shut up, and observe. Of course we were also allowed to take vital signs (namely pulse and blood pressure) and provide any other care necessary under our EMT's or medic's supervision.

This wasn't an exam to ace or a skills test. This was the real deal (or so I thought). I was extremely nervous. As a type A personality I strived to succeed. Such as it was I struggled not to trip over my own two feet.

I think I showed up thirty minutes early, too frightened some random incident would cause me to be tardy, like a plane crash, nuclear reactor meltdown or traffic. No instructions were given to me as to where to show up other than "the building down the street." So I walked into this huge garage and headed over to where a few official looking folk stood.

As reserved as I was the prospect of talking to one of these experienced, professional EMTs was too much for me. Instead I sat and waited and looked lost until someone helped me out. Eventually someone took pity on me and told me who my partners would be for the day.

Gail and Mann. I waited anxiously as I stared at the entrance. I looked for anyone who might fit the description of "older female paramedic and her male partner." For a while I thought I was forgotten about and I would be sitting, waiting forever.

Ten minutes after they were supposed to show up the two strolled in. I shyly introduced myself to the two. Gail was a paramedic. In EMS there are two major levels of care: Advanced Life Support, ALS, and Basic Life Support, BLS. Basic means EMTs and Advanced, Paramedics. Paramedics can do more than EMTs. They can interpret heart rhythms, start IVs, give a lot more drugs, and do more invasive procedures than EMTs.

Though Gail was my training officer she quickly handed me off to Mann. He was friendly and answered my every stupid question. I think Gail mostly tried to ignore I existed.

After getting our ambulance ready we were off! I was terrified. Would we get a woman in labor, a gunshot wound, a stroke, or maybe a car wreck? I had no idea what to expect. What happened next though was something I was fully unprepared for. Six hours of nothing. Yep. We stood by in the parking lot of a hospital for six hours, not moving once.

I was so bored. I asked Mann questions. I studied from my EMT book. I investigated every compartment of the ambulance, eight times. I just about created a brand new nation and culture during those horrendous six hours.

The only thing keeping me awake was the gossip going back and forth between Gail and Mann. Even that was boring since I had no fudging idea who they were talking about.

So when I heard the emergency tones go off, I didn't care if it was a lady in labor, I just needed to get away from that blasted parking lot!

Our run was for a patient with shortness of air. That meant our patient was having trouble breathing! Hurry, hurry, I was thinking. We've got to get there now! However Gail and Mann were not as excited as me and moved way too slowly for my taste. Mann told me though that it is important not to go so fast that you forget to think, that you forget to be safe.

It was a good point and I tried to slow my thinking down. When we got there we found out that our patient was perfectly stable, perfectly okay, but he did have a doctor's appointment he had to go to. My first emergency run and it wasn't even a "true" emergency. (I came to learn "true" emergencies were far in-between at Ryder EMS.)

Though our patient wasn't suffering from anything life threatening I still learned a lot from that run, including how to use the EMS torture device, the stair chair.

Sometimes patients live on the first floor. Sometimes they live on the 22nd, the elevator is broken, and they can't even stand up. How do we get them down to our ambulance? Answer: The Stair Chair. It is a chair with wheels and straps. Two EMS personnel can strap their patient in and take a patient up or down stairs. Sounds good, logical. Except (and I learned this on my first run) it is a lot of work lifting people. No one told me how much you would sweat as an EMT.

The rest of my shift with Gail and Mann was uneventful and far less sweaty, but I sure got to take a lot of vitals signs (pulse and blood pressure)! And with that first twelve hours completed I was halfway done with my ride time.

3 and 4. The Introduction to Ryder EMS, Part Two

I was pumped for my last twelve hours of ride time. I was nearly done with my EMT class. I had finished my eight really intolerably boring hours of Emergency Room observation, and I had already successfully made it through my previous ride time shift.

When I was signing up, there was a small group of us, and I kept volunteering to take a shift, but my instructor kept ignoring me. I was getting more than a bit annoyed. Finally she answered me back in response. "No E.S.T., I want you," her eyes scanned the lineup, "here. Yes, these guys would be perfect for you."

I didn't quite understand why she singled me out to get a specific crew, but I went along with it. That was my general rule. As long as it wasn't idiotic or harmful I would go along. I would simply listen and forgo any judgment. This particular skill certainly aided me in my second shift of ride time.

This time I was on an ambulance, or truck, with two EMTs. I had been told that Basic Life Support (BLS), EMT-only crews were generally busier, but got fewer emergency runs. After my six hour standby and bore-a-thon with Gail and Mann I was positively eager to be and stay busy.

The first EMT was a tall, slightly overweight man of uncertain ethnic origins named Johnson. He was very friendly and apparently held a Masters in Teaching. Perfect for the task of training officer, but yet again my training came primarily from my training officer's partner.

Bentwell was a skinny white male just inches taller than my own height of 5'8". He gave me the once over, asked me a few basic questions, and must have been somewhat impressed. I say this because in those twelve hours he did his best to instruct me as to the inner workings of EMS and Ryder EMS.

Bentwell was a true veteran of EMS. He claimed to be in New York City for 9/11 and in New Orleans in the aftermath of Hurricane Katrina. I could tell he wanted to make sure I knew he had worked "real" EMS. This confused my poor naive mind. He was an EMT working for an EMS organization. Wasn't that real?

He coolly informed me that Ryder was not even close to real EMS, that all we did was "chuck Granny". I didn't understand the term, so rather than show off my ignorance I nodded along. Whatever it was, it didn't sound good.

I sat in the familiar Captain's Chair and we were off for our busy day. It seemed mostly what we did was go up to the hospital floors, not the ER, and take old folks to physical rehab centers or nursing homes. I don't think we had a single "normal" EMS run that day (home to ER).

It was the first time I ever spent in a hospital when I was neither a visitor nor volunteer. I was almost downright respectable. I felt badass alongside these two tried and tested

EMTs. The two also had that sense of flow you only get with a partner you have day in and day out.

Whenever I rode in the back with Bentwell he would question me and instruct me and try to instill any sort of wisdom in my tiny brain. The only question I remember is the one that should stick in every new EMT's head.

He asked me, "What's the single most important thing an EMT can do?"

I ran through every treatment I could possibly think of. CPR? No. AED? No. Oxygen? No. With each negation I grew increasingly anxious. I was failing the test! Finally I grudgingly admitted defeat.

Bentwell smiled and admitted it was a trick question. "The most important thing an EMT can for a patient is to transport them." He paused to let the statement sink in.

'Well duh,' I thought.

He explained further that we can do everything in our power but ultimately our job was to bring them to the doctors in the ER. We can't diagnose. We can barely treat anything, so ultimately the ability to get our patients from point A to point B is our most valuable asset.

Even though I didn't want to admit I overlooked that, I conceded the point. I didn't feel like arguing with Bentwell, particularly since his knowledge far outranked my own.

For a while I thought our day was going to be filled with nothing but transfer runs, but then the emergency tones dropped and our truck number was called. We were needed code three (lights and sirens) to the state fair. I was excited for the potential emergency but also to go to the state fair. I had never had anyone to go to fair with, but now I had work and free admission.

On the way there I learned about the dangers of road rage in an ambulance. Imagine trying to get through rush hour traffic, now multiply that time five and you have what we were trying to get through to get to our destination at the fair.

Now the general rule is to pull over to the right, but any EMT or medic will probably say that they don't care where you go as long as you get the hell out of their way.

I learned a lot on responding to that run. First is that lights and sirens turn intelligent, rational drivers into blubbering idiots. People panic when we come behind them code three, and immediately stop using the big squishy brain thing they were just using a second earlier.

The second thing I learned was that you do not let your anger get the best of you on the road. Because if you do you might grab the PA, which connects to a speaker on the outside of the truck, and scream your head off at the car which got into front of you and just stopped. Just like Johnson did. Bentwell later apologized for the behavior and said it was extremely unprofessional to act in that manner.

I was just excited to go to an emergency where it felt like an emergency. Mann and Gail seemed way too calm to be responding to a real live emergency. Johnson and Bentwell were eager and ready, except it seemed our patient had walked away already. I guess the patient must have felt like his emergency wasn't so dire.

When things settled down towards the end of the night Johnson was finishing up his run report, the bothersome paperwork EMTs and medics are responsible for each patient. Bentwell asked if I knew who the "hero squad" was. I told him I had absolutely no idea.

The Hero Squad, as described by Bentwell, was a group at Ryder EMS who considered themselves heroes and demigods. They were usually folk who had never worked EMS anywhere else and by working at a primarily transfer company had gotten a misconstrued and inflated sense of self.

Bentwell told me it was very important to realize that Ryder was not "true" EMS. At Ryder we rarely worked emergencies, or at least "true" emergencies. And the most severe trauma runs we generally went on involved injuries of the paper cut variety (not even joking-there was a run for a paper cut). The City EMS picked up the serious trauma and emergent runs. I told Bentwell I understood. I wasn't at Ryder because I craved the guts or glory.

I guess I impressed Bentwell enough because he was effusive in his praising on my student evaluation sheet. I think he simply was happy to have someone listen to him and his theories for once.

Ride time was finally complete. All that I had left was to complete my class and pass the national and state examination, easy, when compared to the horrors of Ride time.

5 and 6. The Moo Moo Mover

The time was now. I was no longer a student but a full fledged EMT. I had gone through the interview, the hiring process, and fit for duty test and I was ready for Ryder. I was stoked! I was gonna save lives with my awesome EMT skills! For The City! For America!

But first I had to get through forty eight hours of probation time with a training officer overseeing me. Essentially it was the same as ride time except this time I got to do paperwork! Yay?

I couldn't have asked for a better training officer, Grinyard. Some people just have a knack for teaching and he had it. He saw my nervousness and gently guided me through the murky waters of transfer EMS. Grinyard taught me how to write a good narrative, the name for the story about the patient and what you did for him or her. I learned how to work my radio, how to talk to dispatch and how NOT to talk to dispatch.

From Grinyard's partner, Stevens, I learned that Ryder EMS is full of flawed individuals and that gossip was essential to breathing at Ryder. Whenever Grinyard wasn't teaching me it seemed Stevens was discussing the latest and greatest on the scandals of Ryder.

It seemed the latest issue was this coworker/friend of theirs that was in major debt and stealing money for possibly drug issues. I was starting to feel not as great about my decision to work at Ryder, but it didn't matter. I knew all the gossip! That was the hardest part, right?

In addition to learning my EMT basics and the sexual proclivities of the Ryder EMS workforce I learned that EMS hates fat people. With Grinyard and Stevens I worked on the bariatric ambulance, the truck especially for patients over 400 pounds. I learned that there were many different names for the bariatric truck including The Big Boy Truck, The Fattie Wagon, The Heifer Hauler, and The Moo Moo Mover. Hey, I never said EMTs and medics were particularly nice people.

Patients of an extra large weight seem to give EMS personnel a lot more trouble. They are more difficult to move and lift. They don't fit very well on our tiny stretchers and they sometimes come with a myriad of medical problems.

Most of our patients while I was with Grinyard and Stevens weren't actually bariatric. We only had two or three who technically qualified for our big truck and bigger stretcher.

One of these bariatric patients taught me something else about EMS. EMTs and Paramedics assume pretty much anyone complaining of pain is a drug seeker. The bariatric patient in question was complaining of foot pain. She hadn't had any injury to the foot in question and Grinyard noticed something. The patient stated she was allergic to all non-narcotic pain meds, meaning she said she was allergic to all pain meds that didn't give a high.

But EMTs and Paramedics aren't doctors (though some medics think they are). We can treat to some extent, but we can't diagnose. We transport. It's not our job to decide not to treat someone just because we think all they want is pain medication (though some EMTs/medics do think it's their job).

Grinyard taught me how to work the ambulance and handle patients and paperwork. And Stevens? Stevens taught me that the Boo Boo Bus goes by many names, that Victoria's Secret has a fashion show, and that my time at Ryder EMS may not be fulfilling but at least the gossip would be good.

7. My First Day. His Last.

The training wheels were finally off. It was my first day unsupervised, just my partner and I against the cruel world and I? I did not feel remotely prepared for this opportunity despite all the time spent in preparing for this exact moment.

I was extremely fortunate to go through all this with my best bud from EMT class, Slate. We studied together, carpooled, did orientation together and planned to be on the same shift. Due to our brand new-ness we couldn't be partners, but at least we had someone to talk to when it was over.

Slate and I were nervous but ready to begin, even if when I met my very first solo partner I wanted to run away. My partner was Sketchy, the very guy I spent hours listening to Grinyard and Stevens gossiping about, the one with all the money and possibly drug issues. Oh and what made it even better was that he wanted nothing to do with a new person. I could tell it was going to be a lovely day.

Besides having generally no idea what I was doing or where I was going, the day was going by pretty well. It was Halloween and everyone was in the spirit. Sketchy actually relaxed a bit and offered to answer all my questions.

Everything was okay, until we picked up the obese drug seeker from a rehab facility from the previous week. The lady was complaining of generic pain with no other symptoms. I knew the run was a waste of time, but a run is a run.

We were rolling her to truck when Sketchy asked her if she was short of breath. She said no. I heard her clearly say no. Sketchy freaked out and repeated, "You're short of breath?" She said no, again. I repeated her words to Sketchy, but he had gone nuts. I can't think of another explanation for his subsequent behavior.

He rushed her into the truck and told me to drive code 3, lights and sirens, to the hospital. I had never even seen how to work all the switches necessary, so Sketchy yelled at me which buttons to press and switches to flick. I get moving and faithfully follow my GPS. I follow it so faithfully that I end up on the busiest street on Halloween in the entire city. Every Halloween all the houses on this street really get into their decorating and thus a massive gathering of people line the sidewalk and street. And of course this was during prime trick or treating hours: my first time driving code 3, in the worst possible place and the worst possible time.

So I'm going lights and sirens, inching along in this hugely congested area, pedestrians all over, with Sketchy yelling at me from the back to go faster. I'm about to have a breakdown or run some poor trick or treater over, for a woman who was perfectly fine!

I don't remember anything after getting her to the hospital. In fact I barely remember anything BUT that specific run. Somehow though I survived my first day. I said good night to Sketchy and never saw him again. He didn't show up the next day and was fired later that week. I got to say I didn't spend a single second missing him.

Drugs are bad kids. Stay far away from them and the people who do them.

8. The Fearful Passenger

After the disaster that was the end of my first shift at Ryder EMS I was ready to hang my boots up, turn my hard won uniforms in, and make a quick exit. (I might be a happier, more compassionate, less awful person if I had left Ryder then.) But I am stubborn to a fault and I am not a quitter.

I returned the next day and prayed that Sketchy would not be my partner. Of course I was fortunate in that with Sketchy's dismissal. I hoped for one of the friendly gentlemen I saw the previous day.

My second partner, Humphrey, was one of those unfortunate souls who are not allowed (for whatever reason) to drive the ambulance. The reason why was always varied, like getting into a wreck and being at fault or damaging the truck even slightly or by being under twenty-one. Even having certain violations from driving your personal vehicle could disqualify you from driving the ambulance for awhile.

I am unsure of why Humphrey couldn't drive, but it meant he had to endure a new driver, a brand new driver. I hadn't driven anything larger than a minivan, and that hadn't been for years. I was terrified, plus there is nothing like trying to figure out where you're going during morning rush hour and evening rush hour and lunch rush hour.

Humphrey was crazy or he had to be to endure my driving for twelve hours, but then again he did scream, "Cookies!" a lot, so maybe he was crazy enough.

There is nothing like driving an ambulance to gain an intense knowledge that there are so many asshole drivers and they simply don't care about anyone but themselves. I don't know how but

Humphrey survived that day, though I think I might have claimed three of his nine lives.

9. The Army Guy

There is an interesting connection between EMS and the military. At Ryder EMS we have a lot of people who are either in the reserves, go into the military after working at Ryder, or leave the military and end up working in EMS.

One of my first partners, Atticus, was an ex-Army man who had been out of the military for some time, but kept the haircut and general attitude, which was good for me, a female, but kind of bad for my best gay male bud, Slate.

Our experiences with Atticus were vastly different. When I worked with Atticus he was extremely polite and respectful, patient and kind, as well as a good teacher.

Slate hated working with Atticus. When the two men worked together, Atticus let loose literally. Slate could not stop telling me just how much Atticus farted in the truck both announced and unannounced. Slate also didn't appreciate Atticus's nickname for him, naming him after a popular literary figure (perhaps one that rhymes with hairy otter).

At least we both agreed that Atticus was a good teacher and an important part in making us better EMTs. We never felt hopeless or worried with him, because we knew if things went down Atticus could handle it.

The only thing Atticus couldn't seem to handle was his ex-wife who worked at Ryder EMS, as well as the man she replaced Atticus with. It was a messed up situation and ended poorly for him.

For more on that situation see Chapter 21 from the times I worked with his ex-wife.

10. The Perfect Man

Everyone has flaws. No one is perfect. However Fabio was as perfect as they come. Maybe it was because I was very new and prone to hero worship, but to me Fabio was unassailable in character.

Everything about me and my skills were still largely untested. My driving wasn't very good, worse were my lifting capabilities. I hated being new. No one wants to be partners with a new person.

However not once did Fabio seem upset about being stuck with a new EMT. He was intelligent, kind, gentle hearted and great at his job. He had only been working for five months, but it seemed like he had been an EMT for years.

Like many EMTs at Ryder, Fabio found himself in EMS later in life. Before Ryder, Fabio had been a successful businessman, but burnt out on the fierce competitive nature of that world. It seemed difficult to reconcile Fabio, the gentle EMT, and Fabio, the cutthroat businessman.

Fabio never got frustrated with me or my questions or my failings. He was patient and had an unusually positive attitude for someone working at Ryder or in EMS.

It was with Fabio that I drove code three, lights and sirens, for the second time. The call came from a nursing home for altered mental status, meaning they weren't acting normal. I was driving and instead of expecting me to know exactly what to do he taught me how to drive code three.

No one had taught me all the functions or buttons in the truck. Fabio's calm voice got me to the facility safely, though my heart felt like it was going to pop from chest.

Once we loaded our patient, Fabio still managed to guide me to the emergency room and take care of his patient. I fully don't know remember how I drove us to the ER, only that I got us there and every part of me was covered in sweat. It took twenty minutes for my heart to slow to a normal level.

When Fabio was done with his paperwork he came out and we went through the run. Did we do the best we could? Did we miss anything? Fabio kept complimenting me on my driving. My driving may have actually been crap, but Fabio understood I just needed some reassurance.

Fabio only lasted seven months at Ryder, but to this day he remains in my top five EMTs to work with, and probably number one for all around decent human being.

11. The Negative Nancy

Where Fabio was a positive, uplifting individual, Grey was the complete opposite. Grey was an experienced firefighter and EMT in his late twenties and he hated absolutely everything.

In my years at Ryder, I have noticed how the company took positive, happy people and in just a few short months managed to turn them into disillusioned cynics, but Grey was more than a simple cynic.

I do not know if Ryder was the cause of all Grey's ills like he claimed, but it sure exasperated Grey like none other. When I first worked with him I was still happy with Ryder and my job. The thought that I was getting paid to save lives still made me smile.

I think Grey made it his personal mission to destroy my happiness and "open my eyes" as to what Ryder was really like. "They don't care about you," was a phrase often uttered by Grey to me. I understood the discontentment, but Grey was a perpetual black cloud.

Everything Ryder did was designed to screw you over, according to Grey. Grey's glass wasn't just half empty when it came to his job; it was bone dry. He kept on comparing his job at Ryder to his part time job at a rural county EMS agency.

Which it really isn't fair to compare a busy inner city transfer EMS organization with a tiny, slow county service that only does six hundred runs a year. (For comparison Ryder does about 75,000 runs a year.)

The grass was always greener in this mystic rural county. And everything in The City and at Ryder was shit.

Despite his negativity we got along and I made it my own mission to make him smile. It happened only twice and it was like the sun shone at the dead of night. He left Ryder for a full time job at this verdant mystic place and he was never heard from again.

12. The Scary Bitch

In the course of any sort of job that involves people there are going to be people you like and people you wish never shared air in the same space as you. In EMS this is also true, but if you don't get along with your partner tough luck, because you're stuck with them.

Out of all my partners there have been people I'd rather not work with, but if push came to shove I would get into that truck. There have only been two partners I absolutely refused to work with, and the first was Medusa.

I was still very new and was getting shuffled from partner to partner. I hated that my inexperience still showed, but the only way to get more experience would be to suffer through until the shiny wore off.

My first impression of Medusa was that she hated new people. I know this because she told me when she met me. Medusa was a broad shouldered fierce looking woman in her early forties. Strong women intimidate me and Medusa intimidated the shit out of me.

She explained that she had worked at Ryder for five years, then City EMS for five years, and now she was back at Ryder. I had never ridden with anyone with that much experience before. This woman had seen things I couldn't even fathom at the time.

Our very first run was a City EMS run for a young woman who hadn't taken her psych medications with police on scene. When we got there we were met with an impressively combative, spitting woman in police custody.

It was the first time I restrained anyone, and I was at least grateful I spent so much time practicing how to make restraints. It took three cops, Medusa, and me to get her secured. Even then the woman thrashed about like...well like a mad woman.

I guess Medusa picked up on my nerves because she looked at me and said, "I've got this." A police officer offered to ride in the back with Medusa, but she declined. If it were me I would have had all three cops back there with me.

As I drove I heard the patient scream obscenities and continue to strain at her hopefully tight enough bonds. After five minutes of driving an eerie silence fell in the back of the truck. When I checked my rearview mirror I could see that they were both alive, so the silence was curious.

When we got to the hospital and pulled the patient out of the truck I asked why it got so quiet. My guess was that the crazy lady had tired herself out. Medusa looked at me dead in the eye without even a hint of a smile, piercing me with her gaze, and said, "I threatened her."

Scary scary lady. Medusa was terrifying. Even still I tried to make the best of the rest of our shift. Luckily the rest of the shift was uncomfortable, but survivable. It really wasn't until the next couple shifts with Medusa that she earned her "Bitch" title.

Now I have a flaw (actually several, but this is a bigger one). I don't like women telling me how to do my job. Men, I don't mind as much, but a bossy female will get on my last nerve. Medusa was the epitome of bossy. It stressed me out to no end.

I begged not to be partnered with her, to no avail. The third time I worked with her I was so mad that I couldn't stop crying. Being her partner frayed me, broke me down until I was left counting the seconds until I got off work.

The last time they tried to put us together I threw a fit and refused. My supervisor informed me that I had to, so I stood up for myself for once and said I would go home sick. My supervisor told me I couldn't and threatened to suspend me, and still I held my ground. That was a testament to how much I disliked Medusa. I guess my supervisor finally realized that I wasn't backing down and instead placed me with another EMT who was waiting on a partner. It was really quite an easy fix and yet I got hell for it, but that's how Ryder operated. (Welcome to Ryder EMS, where logic, compassion, and common sense need not apply.)

I never worked with Medusa again, though every time the possibility presented itself I could feel my heart start to hammer in my chest. By the time Medusa left I felt bad for her. She had been working with a new person and hurt her back. Our head boss at the time unkindly informed Medusa that she was too old to be an EMT, and shortly after she was fired supposedly for having too many absences.

13. The Bipolar Chick

EMS seems to attract all sorts of individuals with mental disorders. It makes sense. Only a crazy person would work in EMS, but then there is CRAZY. There are the partners who have some slight eccentricities, and there are the unstable ones who make you feel afraid for your life. You would feel much more comfortable seeing them on your stretcher than in the driver's seat.

MadEyes terrified me to the core. She ranged from really happy to terribly depressed to insanely angry over the course of just a couple of minutes. And that was when she was driving! You didn't know what was going to happen next with her.

There is a general rule in EMS that when you come to work, you leave your outside problems at home. We are professionals. Of course this rule gets broken more than actually followed, but MadEyes was extreme.

On the way to a run downtown MadEyes insisted on stopping by a homeless shelter to try and find her drug addict sister who either ran away or was kidnapped. What made this truly unsettling was that this happened in the very first hour together as partners. Throughout the day I heard MadEyes' entire life story and learned a few things. Her temper was all too short; her road rage prolific.

The end of our shift was as strange as the beginning. We transported a patient dying of cancer from the hospital to his home. His entire family was at home and it was clear that the man didn't have long. My partner busted out sobbing in front of his entire family and didn't stop blubbering for twenty minutes.

Sure it was incredibly sad and I have teared up with certain patients, but I never ever burst out crying in front of my patient or their families.

Another time she got angry at me and decided to curse me out in front of our patients and his wife for no particular reason except that it was a Tuesday.

I was grabbing paperwork on the floor of the hospital and MadEyes went to grab something from the truck. She was fine when she left, but she came back clearly upset and with cry face. When I inquired as to what was wrong she said the elevator dropped and scared her. MadEyes had many fears such as elevators, mucus, and band-aids.

MadEyes crushed my finger under the stretcher one day and I put a band-aid on the offending finger. This was when she informed me as to her queerest fear. She asked me to remove the band-aid and when I refused, all day she gagged out loud whenever she saw the bandaged finger.

Not everyone is made for EMS.

14. The First Regular Partner

We don't want much as EMTs: more pay and fewer hours, except since we can't have that we set our sights lower, maybe a regular partner and a regular truck.

A regular partner means you don't have to play partner Russian roulette. You don't have to worry about being with idiots or new people or annoying people, because you have someone. It's extremely comforting having a regular partner and I was fortunate. It only took me about a month to find one.

We were regular partners for about five months, and I think Lenny was the perfect partner for me at the time. There is so much I can say about the man. We spent every work day together and created a bond which exists even after a year and a half after Lenny left Ryder EMS.

Lenny was my age, and just an inch or two taller than me. He was one of the sweetest men I have ever met and also one of the dopiest.

Lenny did not possess an overabundance of intelligence, but it worked out for us. I was the brains and he the brawns. I was still very new when we first started working together and my biggest weakness, other than my driving which ended up getting taken away from me, was my utter lack of upper body strength.

I remember once we were dispatched on a City EMS call. The patient was in her basement, was about three hundred pounds and said she couldn't walk. The only way out was up a set of stairs, so we got her into a stair chair.

It was an all out struggle getting her up those steps. At one point I lost my balance and ended up with the entirety of the patient's weight crushing one of my knees. I was lucky I had Lenny because I might still be on those stairs, pinned for eternity if not for his strength.

I will admit at times I struggled with Lenny's lack of attention. The first time I worked with him I asked where the ER entrance was for a certain major hospital. At this point Lenny had been working at Ryder for over seven months and still he couldn't tell me.

The only time I absolutely unprofessionally lost my temper in a very public setting was with Lenny. We were being held past our due off time; I was tired and frustrated with Lenny. I often felt like I had to do ALL the thinking in the truck. We had just dropped off in an ER and were taking the stretcher back out to the truck. I was at the feet, guiding the stretcher and Lenny was at the head pushing…or he was supposed to be.

I went to make a turn and then the entire stretcher whipped around and crashed into one of those carts with all the empty collection tubes. The crash made a large noise and the busy ER fell silent. I looked back and saw Lenny holding not the stretcher, but a pile of sheets looking shame faced. He had let go of the stretcher without telling me!

Before I could stop myself I screamed out, "You've GOT TO BE KIDDING ME!" I've never heard an ER quieter than at that moment. I spent the time cleaning up to calm myself then once we were outside I had a calm, rational discussion in which I gently explained that you do not ever let go of the stretcher unless your partner knows that too.

Lenny might have called himself a dummy, but he wasn't. He just had a goldfish memory at times and forgot things easily. I'm somewhat glad I couldn't drive for most of our time together, because at least then I was in control of all the patient care. However Lenny contributed to me having my driving stripped away in the first place.

It was a month after I started. My driving was still rough, but I was getting better. I was driving a patient to a psych facility and got a little too brash in my newfound driving confidence. When pulling around to the entrance I hit the edge of my front right bumper with one of the pillars. Though there were just a few scratches and a small crack in the plastic bumper, Lenny started to freak out.

I was still new, so I followed Lenny's lead. He immediately tattled on me and for that scratch, I had my driving taken away for six months. Little did I know just how often damage like that goes unreported. No one wants their driving taken away.

Apparently Lenny had also been a non-driver just before I started. He backed into a pole in the parking lot of a Taco Bell and did damage to the pole. I did no damage to the pillar, but it was enough for Lenny.

Lenny was good at freaking out. Once he was driving on a highway and we impacted with some giant debris. There was absolutely no way to avoid hitting it. Lenny immediately pulled over and before I even say a word, he was calling to tattle on himself.

There was no damage on the truck at all, but because he told them we were forced back to headquarters to file an incident report and get drug tested.

I think Ryder EMS had an obsession with pee because they would drug test you for anything. Get rear ended, take a pee test. Drop a patient, take a pee test. Get hit in the face by a patient, take a pee test.

Before Lenny worked for Ryder EMS he was at City EMS. To this day I don't know if he was fired or he quit, but his time at City got him obsessed with getting me my first full arrest. I may bitch and moan about Ryder, but at least I didn't have to usually worry about my patients dying. I was fine with the safety of our transfer runs, but Lenny insisted it was important for me.

It was fun to mess with Lenny. Before he knew I was gay, I had him convinced I was dating an "exotic dancer" or more commonly known, a stripper. He would get a funny look on his face and ask me how it was going with the stripper. Unfortunately the stripper and I didn't last for long, just for as long as I got amusement from Lenny, so a few weeks.

I don't know how Lenny dealt with me being gay. I got him to stop yelling "fag" at people in his road rage, without even having to ask him once. I think while I saw him as another brother, he fell in love with me a bit.

For a long time everyone, except Slate, thought Lenny and I were dating. Lenny was constantly referred to as my boyfriend and one repeat patient of ours thought we were married. Lenny didn't help the gossip, because he would always pitch a fit when they tried to split us up. It was sweet, and unlike other coworkers Lenny never asked me out or made me feel uncomfortable. However for a while I was getting some very odd drunk texts from him, asking why was I messing with him. I brought them up to Lenny and he didn't honestly remember sending them.

I shared a lot with Lenny: my personal drama, inside jokes, and many hugs. Even after Lenny left Ryder to work transportation inside a local hospital whenever I saw him he would sweep me off my feet in a bone crushing hug.

The other advantage to having a regular partner was the greater likelihood of having a regular truck. In fact Lenny and I only managed to get one because no one else wanted the blasted thing.

Our ambulance was awful; that is true, but I did everything I could to make it decent. Lenny would constantly bitch about it, but it was nice for me knowing where everything was in the back of my ambulance.

We also decorated it. We joked that Ryder was more like UPS, because we have people sign off to receive packages so we made stickers and badges, which read, "R-UPS". For months after Lenny left our R-UPS sticker could still be found in our truck.

Lenny could be a bit dimwitted, but that was usually easily dealt with. The only thing I couldn't deal with at all was his temper, even though in saying so I am giant hypocrite. I didn't quite break any clipboards in rage while working with Lenny, but certainly not for lack of trying. (I have since mellowed a tad.)

Lenny however did break stuff when she was angry. Once when our stretcher wouldn't lock into place in the back of the ambulance, he got outrageously angry. He slammed the stretcher into the locking mechanism so hard he bent the stretcher such that it couldn't lock into place in *any* truck. We had to go to headquarters and get a new stretcher. Lenny's rage was terrifying as well as his road rage. Boy needs to take up yoga or something.

But for the most part he was my loveable, dopey buddy. He was my first regular partner and he will always hold a place in my heart.

You can't work with someone (willingly) for five months in an ambulance together without loving him or her like a family member (or at least one you still talk to).

15. The Goofball

Some people do not simply give a fudge. Jester was one of those people. He didn't care what dispatch, supervisors, his fellow coworkers or what the lay person thought of him.

He often came into work late, often hung-over, due to nights spent drinking and playing video games. He loved to blast pop music from the speakers drowning out the incessant radio traffic from dispatch.

One time when Jester went to grab some lunch, he decided to grab a sandwich from a downtown shop. The problem was there was nowhere to park the ambulance, so Jester demonstrated how much he cared by putting on his emergency lights and blocking a lane of traffic.

He wore dress shoes to work instead of ankle high boots, against regulations, simply because he didn't feel like buying boots. He was happy and relatively carefree. He was laid back, almost to a fault but everyone loved him.

In fact I think my first regular partner had a bit of a man crush on him. Lenny always lamented not getting to ride with Jester more, and was jealous when I or Slate got to ride with him.

He hit on every woman he met shamelessly, and without getting to know the women invited them out to dinner. Jester was not very successful, but definitely not for lack of trying.

Jester was one of those people who brightened every room he entered, but his time at Ryder was short lived. Shortly after I got to work with him, he joined the Army, because interestingly enough he wanted structure in his life.

16. The Puerto Rican

I hate to profile, but Ricardo was a fierce, extremely fiery Puerto Rican. I know this, because he had a habit of saying so to anyone he talked to.

No one liked working with Ricardo. He was an asshole, never stopped talking, was arrogant, a constant complainer, a sexist, homophobe, and an overall prick.

I was fortunate to only have gone out with Ricardo for a single run. It was a backup 911, City EMS, run for ankle pain. On the drive there I pleaded for death to come swiftly or to at least be rendered deaf, so I wouldn't have to listen to his inane prattle anymore. It was at times like that I wished I was a bitch so I could have told him to shut up.

Ricardo was very...shall we say confident and took charge of my run. Though it bristled against my control freak nature I allowed him to do his thing while I recorded all the patient's information.

I officially stopped giving Ricardo a chance when he made a homophobic statement in front of our patient. I'll give him that he didn't know that I was gay, but I will not tolerate that kind of hate speech (of any nature) in front of a patient.

The patient may have shared similar views with Ricardo. I don't know, but I do know that Ricardo's comment made the patient very uncomfortable. Ricardo simply had no sense of when to shut the hell up.

He was semi-tolerable when taken in tiny doses and generally he was nice enough, but when he transferred out of The City I was not sad to see the homophobic prick go.

17. The Lazy Bum

There are some people who have worked at Ryder EMS for years and still are as diligent about patient care as ever. And then there are the ones who play the system and abuse the freedom that the job allows. Garfield was of the second variety.

He gave not a single crap about Ryder, dispatch, his partners, or even his patients. Garfield enjoyed the privileges of seniority with seemingly none of the responsibilities. He was one of the many training officers, but I heard from many of his students that he didn't teach them a lick. He even ran off at least one new hire with his attitude.

But you see, Garfield had charm. Many a man has gotten away with murder, all because he knew how to charm a crowd. So Garfield got away with his actions time and time again.

I only worked with him once. I was waiting on a partner. Garfield was enjoying being "special" by working supply. The supply office is responsible for issuing trucks and equipment each day. Working in supply is a privilege due to the fact that it's a nice break from having to do runs and deal with annoying patients. Supply tended to be a much more relaxed environment than "the streets". Few EMTs get to work supply because those that typically do, the supply techs, get paid less than EMTs. Why pay an EMT to do the job of a lesser wage employee?

While I was waiting for a partner a long distance run came out. The Powers That Be convinced Garfield to work with me and do the run. He said the only reason he did it was because our destination was his stomping ground. I was just glad to be done waiting for a non-existent partner. I was also happy to get a run which took us out of The City. Usually only "special" crews get long distance runs.

We went out in Garfield's regular truck. He refused to go out in anything else. We picked up the patient. The ride took about two hours and was perfectly uneventful. We dropped off the patient. Now at this point you grab some food, because dispatch can't breathe down your throat out of the radio contact, and food is important. Or it's even acceptable, if the transport time was long enough, to sit down and eat, and spend some time outside your truck.

What is not acceptable is what Garfield did. First we sat down to eat, and then he went shopping for an hour in a pet store. I was chomping at the bit to head back to The City. If I were a driver at that point I might have went back without Garfield. Garfield seemed unconcerned about our atrociously long down time.

When we finally got back in the truck and started back, Garfield decided he didn't want to do another run. He called the supervisor and told her he had to rush home because the ceiling in his bathroom at home collapsed and hit his fiancée. The story was true but greatly exaggerated. A bit of drywall conked his fiancée, but she was more than fine. So Garfield got off when we got back to the city with no repercussions.

I'm pretty easy going, but I about had an aneurysm at Garfield's actions. I do not care what a person's view on Ryder is, you show up to work. It *is* what we get paid crap money to do.

18. The "Real" EMT

Sometimes through a mixed up series of events an EMT who worked for a 911 service for an extended period of time will find him or herself at Ryder EMS. These poor, unfortunate individuals have never worked for a transfer service, so when they do get the full Ryder experience they are fully unprepared.

Rico Suave was one such soul. He was squabbling with the county service where he worked at and due to a matter of politics found himself in need of a job. Ryder, with its inability to hold onto their employees for typically more than six months, is always hiring! So Rico Suave found himself at Ryder.

Rico Suave had many positive attributes. He was handsome, intelligent, eager, a good EMT, friendly and a sweet talker. Rico Suave was fun to hang out with and had some hilarious stories, but Rico Suave had one major problem. And that problem, of course, was Ryder EMS.

Rico Suave could not help but compare Ryder and his county service. He wanted to be an active helper. He wanted to use his skills and save lives. It is a great goal and desire, but one that will go largely unfulfilled at Ryder. When your day is nonstop transfers from hospitals to nursing homes likely the only skills you will use are your ability to take a pulse and blood pressure.

I felt bad for Rico Suave. It was clear he didn't fit in at Ryder and he missed his old service. So when his old service finally asked him back I was sad to see such a great, funny guy go, but was pleased to see him smiling like he was when he first started at this accursed company.

19. The Canadian

With my many partners I have ridden with a diverse group, diverse in personality, race, gender, orientation, education and economic status. But it wasn't until I rode with Cannuck that I got to ride with someone from a foreign country: Canada!

To my American disappointment she didn't say, "Eh," after every word, only once in a while. She did say "about" as "aboot" though to my impish glee.

Cannuck had worked in EMS in Canada for a number of years. Somehow she ended up married to a guy in our state, with him taking divinity classes at a local conservative seminary.

One of the first things I learned about Cannuck was that she had a twin, a gay twin. Cannuck struggled with this because how could one twin be gay and the other not? She did not understand her sister's orientation, but it was clear Cannuck loved her sister very much.

Cannuck held her place wedged firmly between two people: her husband and her sister. I'm not sure how she managed that feat. How do you stay Switzerland when a person you love is pulling on each of your arms, pulling you apart?

This woman, in the same year, went to her twin's very gay Canadian wedding, and to her husband's master of divinity graduation at a school where fire was invented purely for the gays and other unbelievers. I will admit at first I was upset with Cannuck for not being an advocate for marriage for gay folk. I mean she went to her lesbian sister's wedding!

But not all of us are surrounded by friends or family who support our choices. It is a delicate balance Cannuck strives to achieve. I may disagree, but I have to give her props. It takes a certain amount of strength to stay balanced, and I will admit I do not envy the task.

20. The Shameless Flirt

There are some women who as a part of their personality can't seem but flirt with any potentially available man they see. They are a dime a dozen. Perhaps more notable are the married men who do the same.

Married Man, M.M., was so consistently overly affectionate with women, freely giving out hugs to any around that my first thought was that he was gay. Surely no straight man would be that affectionate and friendly with nearly every single woman he encountered.

I was soon proven wrong when the first time I worked with him and he found out I liked women, he pointed out EVERY SINGLE woman he found attractive. This of course was every woman he laid eyes on. My next thought was that this was a painfully single, straight man.

Again I was proven wrong when M.M. started to mention his anniversary plans with his wife. I couldn't understand it. Surely this crazy women loving man wasn't married. I mean he flirted all the time and was always in some fashion touching his female coworkers. How could any wife be okay with that?

Then one day I, along with several other coworkers, got a rather creepy text from M.M. talking about "my body" and how I "make him forget his wife." It was quite disturbing, particularly before I realized the message wasn't sent just to me.

I mean, what the hell? When confronted about the text, M.M. quickly replied that it was a joke that he and his partner for the day came up with. I wondered if his wife would be so amused.

21. The Obnoxiously Chipper One

I am very much not a morning person, and I really don't understand anyone who is. Additionally I am a very controlled, self contained individual, so it was with utter dismay that I endured Tweety and her exceedingly chipper personality.

In such a close knit community like Ryder EMS, the gossip network tends to be extreme and ludicrous. For a few months people at Ryder were convinced I was dating Lenny, despite my unabashed homosexuality. Also I was said to be currently in medical school or even already a doctor. I'm not sure how someone works full time as an EMT and does those things, but I digress.

The gossiping at Ryder was vast and still mostly centered around a small number of people, of which Tweety was one. It wasn't difficult to see why when you heard that her ex-husband,

Atticus, and her current boyfriend both worked at Ryder. Ryder is a big company, but not THAT big.

Despite her personal troubles, Tweety always gave the impression of exuberance. Seemingly nothing could faze her, not even when both Atticus and her boyfriend were fired for issuing death threats against each other and fighting at work.

By the time I worked with Tweety both Atticus and her boyfriend were long gone, and another ex-Ryder employee filled the void. All the drama can be interesting but when I was told I would be working with Tweety, all of it ceased to matter. My only thoughts then were centered on how long I would be able to endure eternal happiness.

Once I got to work with Tweety a few times and found how her happiness was NOT eternal, and in fact frustration and anger were common I found that it was easy to get along with her.

The only major thing besides that extreme chipperness I had difficulties with was the dipping. Smoke 'em if you got them but please do not dip! I really rather not deal with your tobacco spit in various containers in the ambulance, especially coke bottles. I used to like coke. Love it even. But after one extremely tragic accidental swig of Tweety's bottle I will NEVER drink coke again...I hate dippers.

22. The Example

When you first start working at Ryder you look at those long-timers and are in awe of their experience, the way they hold themselves and joke with ease about morbid topics.

A few months later when you start to hate everything that there is to hate about Ryder EMS, you start to see those people differently. You wonder what kind of person would endure this abusive treatment for one year, let alone three to five years.

Shoot, a three to five year sentence at Ryder sounds worse than prison. You wonder just how insane these people are. I mean what sane person would endure such frustrations and aggravations for more time than they absolutely had to?

Either you have to be a saint, an asshole who needs to be treated poorly so he can be an asshole, or you need to be insane. Gollum was one of the insane ones. By the time I met him he had been at Ryder EMS for over three years, and it clearly had made him unstable.

Working with him was at times terrifying. You never knew when he might go off. His favorite person to yell at was his wife, on the phone, while he was driving, when your only option for escape was to throw yourself bodily from the vehicle into oncoming traffic.

But sometimes that wasn't good enough for Gollum. One time he drove to his place and started to have an argument with his wife, while I sat helpless in the truck outside. I guess that wasn't enough for them because they brought it outside. I was just about to take the truck and leave when he rushed in and sped away as his wife came towards the truck.

When Gollum wasn't yelling at his wife he had this eerie, kind of creepy, quiet fatherly air about him. He reminded me of those cartoon villains with the glasses whose eyes you can't see due to the glare that comes from within apparently because this phenomenon is present even in the dark.

Despite Gollum's longevity at Ryder EMS it seemed even he had his limits. Gollum started interviewing for jobs and finally ended up where I'm sure all Ryder EMS employees will end up: a psychiatric facility. Granted Gollum was working there and not a patient, but I feel it's just about the same thing.

To me, Gollum became the utmost prime example to keep your time at Ryder EMS as brief as possible.

23. The Majestic

It is amazing how some people can stand removed from their actions, like it doesn't touch them. They have an aura surrounding them which sets them apart from their compatriots.

The Queen was just that, or at least she reminded me of one with her demeanor. And I'm not talking about bossiness or superiority. She never seemed to slouch and I don't think she truly walked, but strode everywhere she went. A part of her majestic nature I think came from her carefully measured words and unflappable sense of self.

You never knew where you stood with her as she regarded you with cool, half lidded eyes. She might joke with you and she was certainly friendly, but she always struck me as different from the common folk around her.

I think I may be the only one to consider The Queen in this way. Maybe she only acted in this manner when we worked together and when I happened to be around. She was a dedicated, fierce single mother with her share of heartbreak.

I don't know how it is possible but she even managed to class up discussing Channing Tatum's physique and the crude and kind of awful movies currently in theaters.

One time a rumor got around that I didn't like working with The Queen. When The Queen confronted me about this I felt like a lowly peasant brought in by her guards, forced to report to her majesty. I struggled to convince her that the rumor was completely false (which it definitely was) and when we came to an understanding I felt myself being dismissed.

She may have intimidated me slightly, but she had that spark that you sort of want for yourself. But if you couldn't copy her style, at least any time spent in her company was spent amongst royalty.

24. The Buddha

It takes a very patient, laid back person to last a year working at Ryder EMS. To deal with the horrendous amount of involuntary overtime hours worked, the low pay, the piss poor benefits, and the general vile treatment we endure from patients, nurses, and our own command staff. It takes a saint to not lose your temper at Ryder. Now imagine the type of person it takes to work nearly thirty years at Ryder. It takes the Buddha.

Mr. Buddha is as close to the Buddha in personality as I have ever seen. He is the most Zen human being I have ever met. Mr. Buddha did not express any sort of emotion. Nothing made him angry or happy or really anything but passive. He was the unbroken sea; nothing could disrupt those waters.

Mr. Buddha and I formed a fast accord. I think in part I reminded him in part of his regular partner. It also helped that I was a non driver, as Mr. Buddha preferred to drive all day. But if he was stuck in the back all day, he didn't complain. He never complained.

Mr. Buddha was quiet, but certainly not unapproachable. It was difficult to get to know Mr. Buddha, but he was always interested in my life. He was extremely intelligent. He knew The City inside and out and while I was struggling to navigate the highways and how to get to all the ERs, Mr. Buddha hardly ever took the highways. Instead he favored all the tiny back roads you have never heard of and will never heard of ever again.

There was a distinct peace when I worked with Mr. Buddha. No matter how angry I got at the new idiotic thing dispatch did, he would just sigh and say, "Oh well." I then felt like a fool for my overreaction and attempted to be Zen like Mr. Buddha.

The major things I learned about Mr. Buddha were only gleaned from reading between the lines. That's how I learned that he was a devout Catholic, so amazingly intelligent, used to work in dispatch, did not want to ever be a supervisor, was dissatisfied with the company, and was gay.

Mr. Buddha talked about leaving Ryder EMS even to go work somewhere like a grocery store or going back to dispatch. But every time I would follow up with Mr. Buddha on these plans, he would demur and never talk about anything solid.

When Ryder took away our names and gave us each a prisoner number, I mean employee number; our newest employees were in the thousands and Mr. Buddha's? Mr. Buddha had a single digit number.

Mr. Buddha was in so many ways Ryder EMS. I have often wondered what he was like when he was young and impressionable. I heard a rumor that when Mr. Buddha was young he was having...we'll say sexual relations with one of the big bosses. How could this be? The Mr. Buddha I knew was an asexual creature of saint like proportions.

One time when I was working with him I unintentionally used a slang word and he asked me about the word. I joked that I would give him a slang dictionary, but then I actually bought one for him. I tried to give it to him, but he refused my gift. He said he preferred to be ignorant.

Another thing about Mr. Buddha was that even though he had more seniority than even the command staff, he didn't use it at all. It was true that he was given a regular truck, but it wasn't a new truck, just an okay one, and if he wasn't given that truck he might inquire about it, but would accept any truck given to him.

If he really wanted he could have had any plumb spot in Ryder, but he worked the streets in the most over worked division of Ryder. Mr. Buddha was an enigma and I spent many shifts trying, unsuccessfully to figure him out.

25. The Despised One

It seems that in every workplace there is that one person that no one wants to work with. Everyone unanimously makes the decision that this individual is truly horrendous and is ostracized from the group as a whole. It's all very high school and yet is very pervasive in our lives after high school.

For quite some time at Ryder there was Fungus. Besides Mr. Buddha, who could put up with anything, no one wanted to ride with Fungus. Fungus was legend at Ryder; such were the stories and rumors about him.

Everyone wanted to justify why they didn't want to work with him and why he was deserving of such derision. The rumors went from the small, "he smells," to the fantastical, "pretty sure he's a serial killer." Mostly it seemed that no one wanted to work with him because he surpassed people's "weird limit."

It was amazing the lengths people went to not have to work with Fungus. Mostly they tried to keep Mr. Buddha and Fungus together, but varying circumstances left Fungus without a partner.

The mental breakdowns people went through when they were told in no uncertain terms that they had to work with Fungus were both dramatic and entertaining.

To me Fungus did seem odd and perhaps a bit off-putting, but I never could match Fungus to his legend. So when it was my turn to be sacrificed and be his partner I went without much fuss.

Certain things I found out about Fungus matched the rumors, like he certainly did not smell good and probably needed a shower or two. However beyond his inability to talk like a "normal person" he wasn't that bad.

I think a lot of people struggled with him because he was an unabashed geek and nerd. He couldn't relate to many of his coworkers because he'd rather marathon video games than go out in the sunshine.

Another possible reason for how Fungus achieved his reputation was that Fungus was creepy at times and that he thought he was much more intelligent that he actually was. He would spout out these theories and ideas, which were interesting, but also a lot of bunk. Even with this flaw and his unnerving personality Fungus still ranked above several other partners I've been stuck with.

I guess to each his or her own, but unlike my coworkers who withered away in Fungus' presence I stood tall. He wasn't my kryptonite.

26. The Privileged

There is nothing like being put in an ambulance with someone who adamantly doesn't want to be in one. Synopsis: it blows a big one.

I was waiting on a partner, but there was no one coming in for at least six hours. If there existed kind souls at Ryder EMS they might have let me go home, but not a single kind soul was found that day.

After two hours of waiting partnerless they took an EMT working in the supply office and sent us out for a couple of runs. Barbie, my partner, was absolutely furious. She made it crystal clear that she didn't want to be working on the streets with me or at all.

Barbie explained her situation. Her regular partner was a medic, who was on vacation. Since Barbie didn't want to ride with anyone besides her medic, she chose to work in supply, off the streets, an option given to very few individuals.

Barbie spent the two hours we were together unleashing a torrent of abuse towards Ryder EMS. I couldn't do much but attempt to quell the irate woman I was stuck with.

Despite all the promises that she would only have to do one run, in a brand new ambulance and all she had to do was drive, she still bitched incessantly.

By the end of our time together I couldn't tell who was more grateful for it to be over. They let Barbie go home and as for me they sent me back out with someone new. Oh to be a privileged bitch. What a dream!

27 and 28. The Lucy Truck

My first introduction to the Lucys was during a run my first regular partner, Lenny, and I did. We called for lift assist and when Lenny heard the unit responding he got all excited. "The Lucy Truck!" he exclaimed with a certain amount of glee. When my dumbfounded face didn't clue Lenny into curing my confusion I finally asked, "Who or what is the Lucy Truck?"

Lenny explained. The Lucy Truck was a pair of regular partners, both with the first name of Lucy. Apparently they were both awesome as well. Though initially doubtful I soon came to see the amazing nature of both Lucys.

It is surprising that I have worked with them both separately, because they very rarely were ever torn asunder. In fact they would pitch a bit of a fit whenever faced with this scenario.

I can't say I blame them. Riding with someone new always leads to awkwardness and other similar "first date" scenarios.

Though I rode with each of them I mostly got to know them outside the confining walls of the ambulance. Lucy A. and I were extras in a movie, a very odd movie involving a goth circus. With both of them I have walked many an interestingly themed 5K: Color, Glow, Clown, you name it and they were there.

Lucy B. and I bonded over a double shift worked together and the haunted truck which made eerie noises at 3 in the morning.

The two had been partners for over a year when I started. That type of longevity was difficult to find in my division. The Lucy Truck was an institution. I didn't think I'd be at Ryder for long enough to see their dissolution, but then Lucy B went part time and all of Ryder EMS mourned the demise of the Lucy Truck.

29. The Player

I think there is a special bond formed between classmates in EMT class. Slate and I were in class five days a week for two straight months. We had a small class and it was pretty easy to form lasting friendships, besides the few crazies. Our class produced a number of EMTs and several came to work at Ryder EMS.

Gosling was actually one of my classmates that I never did hang out with much. I remembered him being intelligent with a good body and a handsome face. Once we both started at Ryder I would chat with him when I saw him and kept up with his life.

As Gosling became more comfortable at Ryder he started to develop an attitude, both condescending and cocky. Strangely I never really minded his attitude. I think it was the fact that he didn't treat me like I was stupid. He knew for a fact I wasn't. He was second in our EMT class, second only to me.

While I pursued my dream of medical school, Gosling was getting his pre-requirements for nursing school. We understood each other. So when we worked together I wasn't surprised to find we got along fine.

Perhaps a bit surprising were the stories Gosling told me. Gosling was a hot guy with a decent job and smart. He was a catch and Gosling knew this and exploited it. I listened to his crude crusades to the popular bars in The City and the women he…oh let's not sugar coat…the women he fucked.

It seemed every time we worked together he had new stories to tell. It took all my composure to keep my jaw from dropping and my face from blushing. This was my arrogant asshole friend. I had to play it cool. But man, fathers raise your girls right and hopefully they won't end up one of Gosling's conquests.

30. The Ditz

As a woman who was raised to believe in the importance of intelligence and the strength inherent in intelligence, I struggle sometimes with other women. Women who either pretend to be stupid or whom willfully struggle with intelligence; well I don't know how to deal with them. I will admit sometimes they say things which either make me want to shake them until the candy comes out, or cry uncontrollably over the state of the world today.

Of course we have more than a few of these women at Ryder EMS, but one in particular I think reigns supreme.

I have many coworkers who will talk about uncomfortable social and political issues mostly because they feel they are correct in their views. (I won't lie. I do this sometimes.) However Mitzy had a tendency to say insensitive things without ever meaning to.

It was hard to dislike Mitzy. Truly hating her was like hating a puppy. It knows not what it does. She could get frustrated at Ryder just as easily as anyone else, but I never saw her be mean to anyone ever.

She and her regular partner were well known for perhaps several reasons, but for me the most notable were the prank wars they had. The war started out as water fights with saline flushes, and messing with each other's trucks, but soon progressed.

I will always remember the night Slate and I headed out to the parking lot and saw a curious sight. Someone's car was completely covered in sheets graffitied with such witty sayings and dick pictures. At first I was horrified and confused, but when I learned it was one of the prankster's cars, the pieces all fell into place.

Some folk didn't like Mitzy due to the favoritism she received, but when the new boss started and that fell away it wasn't that hard to get along with her once more. We may not have all that much in common, but despite her uninformed words, I'll take her as my partner any day.

31. The Quiet Racist

Before my job at Ryder EMS I had very little exposure to the poorest members of our society. I was isolated from it by growing up in the suburbs and then later in a private college in a small town. Anyone of a different race I encountered was just as or more intelligent than I was.

As such I was unprepared to go into the homes of the poorest people of The City and experience the different cultures. But I was raised to hate racism, so I did.

At first glance, Strummond seemed like a stoic, but friendly young man who rarely let anger get the best of him. He and I got along well and had similar tastes in music. For awhile my only complaint about Strummond was that he operated at a much slower pace than my impatient nature would have liked.

Then seemingly out of nowhere the comments started. Strummond started cursing out the Mexicans and once the comments started they always managed to pop up now and then. It was difficult to see this unsavory side of Strummond. To me Strummond was still the friendly man who helped me look for a new car and joked around with me.

At the time I didn't understand why Strummond felt the way he did. Unfortunately after working at Ryder EMS for over two years I believe I do. It's time for some perhaps unwarranted honesty. It is hard to work in a city for EMS and not develop racist feelings. Due to my penchant for intellectual analysis, I have struggled to figure out why.

I don't know for certain where Strummond's feelings came from, but I have thought of a possibility. As a rule EMS don't care for poor people. They call for ambulances for the slightest of reasons, because they don't have cars or rides and they would rather not pay for a taxi or the bus. As a general rule EMTs and medics don't like responding to these non-emergent scenes. In their eyes if a taxi will easily replace us, then we are needed elsewhere. Also it tends to be among the poorest who abuse the emergency services.

Another reason why EMS don't like the poor is because some of their homes border on inhabitable, and sometimes are completely inhabitable. At these residences we encounter awful sights and smells. All of this we endure in the most dangerous areas of our cities, risking our lives to help others.

For me though I don't enjoy going to certain areas of town and certain domiciles, if the reason for the 911 call is legit and everyone uses their manners then I'm okay.

However it seems for some of the poorest members of society (not counting the homeless- their manners are usually decent) there is no reason to be kindly to the people attempting to help.

I would like to say I fight against treating anyone differently just because of the color of their skin or the contents of their wallet, and I do. But if I give no attitude and am given one in turn then my friendly nature gets downgraded to a strained polite professionalism. We simply do not get paid enough to suffer attitude when all we want to do is help.

So while I understand Strummond now, I still disagree with his wholesale view of certain races. However I think it's fair to say that while working in EMS hasn't turned me into a full blown racist, it has definitely made me classist. (Though working with the rich comes with its own set of problems. In EMS we prefer hard working, tough, respectful middle class folk as our patients. But then again they aren't the ones who usually call 911.)

32. The Night Shift Queen

Dayshift was my bread and butter. I had been working it for two months and I knew generally what to expect on a daily basis. However I wanted to make a few extra dollars. I could have picked up another dayshift, but the thought of working a double intrigued the masochistic part of me.

A straight twenty four hours of work. It seemed like an insane notion, so of course I was drawn to the idea. So I worked my normal dayshift and then didn't go home; I went back to headquarters and they placed me with a night shift partner.

To me night shift was a bit intimidating. The dangerous city in darkness, my partner, Taffy, seemed unfazed by the dangers lurking behind every street corner. She was a long-timer in the division, which meant she had been there for about three years, most of it on night shift.

Now at night there are typically no discharges off the hospital floors or annoying doctor's appointments. In fact the only runs done at the dead of night are psych transfers, transfers out of ERs, City EMS runs, and dialysis runs.

There is a generally quiet period during the night, 2am-4am, which is then broken by The Renal Roundup, a phrase coined by night shifters so long ago that no one knows its true origins. The Renal Roundup is used to describe the number of regular patients taken for their early morning dialysis.

Taffy, hearing I was working a double, continually urged me to take a nap. How could I take a nap at work? Wasn't that illegal? When Taffy brought out her computer to watch a movie, that's when I truly realized what a different beast night shift was.

Night shift seemed incredible. On dayshift we ran our butts off with hardly a break to even eat during our twelve hours. In fact there were several times I didn't eat due to how busy and rushed we were.

Night shift runs were generally short with actual standbys in between runs. Rush was not in Taffy's lexicon, and we did everything slowly. Not used to the pace, I found myself fighting not to bounce off the walls of the ambulance. It was too slow. There was too much downtime.

Taffy seemed to be important in the world of nighttime at Ryder EMS. She would regularly call up dispatch just to chat! I was scandalized. No one calls dispatch to chat. Their time was sacred! Besides they were the enemy. But here was Taffy teasing my least favorite dispatcher and calling him by his first name! I didn't even know he had a first name. It seemed too informal to for him to have one.

Night shift was so casual I found myself wanting some starch for my uniform just to make sure that the night shift lackadaisical attitude didn't seep into my absolute and complete professionalism. It would be a long while before I relaxed enough to see the benefits of night shift, about a year later when I was forced to quit or go to night shift in order to take a single class.

The Night Shift Queen in the end met her match in Ryder's immorality. When Taffy was pregnant and her doctor put her on bed rest, Ryder fired her, because that is just the type of wonderful company that Ryder is.

33. The Cursed Ginger

I don't mean to knock on gingers. I have cousins who are red headed (that's the equivalent of "I have a gay friend" right?). I only make fun of Rusty because the two major events which resulted in a patient getting hurt in all my time at Ryder were when I was working with him.

After Lenny, my partner at the time, left I had no regular partner, so for the most part I was either partnered up with someone random or one of the handful of people on my shift. I was still unable to be partnered with my buddy Slate, so that left Rusty who generally either rode with me or Slate.

Don't get me wrong. Rusty was an alright guy and I got along with him decently, but we lacked chemistry as partners and as a result, communication. So much can go wrong when you don't communicate well with your partner.

I say Rusty was cursed because mishaps' happened around him. Besides the occasional driving mishap and a couple totally unjustifiable complaints from patients I have been a mediocre to stellar employee. Twice with him though things happened that shouldn't have. No one died, but I can't deny that no one got hurt.

The first was not really either of our faults and I deemed it to be a fluke. The second was a result of anger, exhaustion, a difficult life, a difficult patient, and THE CURSE!

Rusty was the type of person who is so laid back and relaxed that he didn't really do serious nor did he understand some basic facts about driving the ambulance. One of those is that you cannot drive an ambulance the same way with a patient in the back than without one.

Not a single soul has ever said ambulances were designed with a patient's comfort in mind. Every single little bump you feel as a driver is magnified in the back tenfold. Every slightly sharp curve you make throws your partner into your patient's lap. Every sudden stop shoves your partner into the "safety net" designed to hang stethoscopes and for your bad driving.

Rusty didn't understand ANY of this. I blame the fact that most of his formative months as an EMT were spent as a driver for Slate or me. He never really got a chance to feel what it is like to be tossed around the back of an ambulance like a rag doll.

I try and make it a rule to never ever yell at anyone while at work. I might raise my voice, but I don't generally scream or yell. We were transporting a patient on a backboard. I was a bit stressed and I was very concerned for our patient. Rusty made a hard stop and our patient nearly flew off the stretcher. I raised my voice and told Rusty to never make a stop like that with a patient on a backboard. Get this. He laughed! That rat bastard laughed. I lost it. I screamed, "It's not a joke! You NEVER DO THAT AGAIN!" Rusty was cowed. Afterwards he apologized profusely, and that was good, but more importantly he never did that again.

Rusty also had this awful habit of not thinking before he spoke. I didn't mind so much as long as it was just the two of us. It drove me nuts however when patients were involved.

A single example of the multitude was one time we were picking up a cancer patient from chemo treatment. Before we moved him Rusty noticed lots of hair on the patient's pillow. Immediately before thinking he said, "Did he get a haircut?" The patient's wife simply said no. Then Rusty continued to make it better, by saying, "Really, cause that's a lot of hair." It didn't occur to Rusty until much much later the hair-falling-out properties of chemo drugs and his incredible case of foot-in-mouth disease.

34. The Overly Dramatic One

Before in The Player, chapter 29, I talked about the bonds that form between classmates. We suffered through countless hours of instruction and worked together to learn skills and get ready for the state and national tests.

Unstable, one of my classmates, actually didn't pass the class the first time, but managed to get through on her second. So by the time she started to work at Ryder, I had already worn off my "newness". Almost as soon as she started the rumors surrounding her started as well.

There were the basic ones that surround every new person: can't lift, doesn't know anything, and can't drive. It's honestly more exceptional when a new person can do any of those things, than if they can't. Those rumors I usually ignore. However new rumors started labeling Unstable as emotionally bonkers and exceedingly overdramatic.

It wasn't a pleasant emotion I was feeling when I was told she would be my partner for the day. But as always I tried at the very least not to ruin the day before it started. Unstable though came into the truck bawling her eyes out.

I won't lie. Strong emotions freak me out. I could have ignored her, but we were trapped in a metal box together and once we were in class together and chatted on a daily basis. So I asked what was wrong, and wow I don't think she stopped talking the entire day.

I survived, but that's all that could be said for working with Unstable. Since then she has gone part time to take a paramedic class, so you know God Help Us All.

35. The Drag Strip Queen

One benefit to working at Ryder EMS versus the over so popular City EMS is that we get to work "specials". Specials are events such as concerts, festivals, and sporting events that use us as medical assistance. These events are popular because usually all you do is sit, enjoy a free show, and hand out band-aids.

It is hard to get off "the streets" to work a special unless you're a "special" person, so you work them on your days off. I was eager to get a foot into the "special" racket, but my options were limited. Due to my non-driving status all I could work were events with another EMT which were few. Due to the advanced nature, most specials wanted at least one medic.

So when I found a special for two EMTs I jumped on the opportunity. It was to be medical assistance for a drag racing strip just outside The City. I was nervous to work such an event with my limited trauma experience, but I wanted to work a special and this was my only option.

On my off Saturday, I woke up early and walked into work. I was wondering what my partner would be like, as most people who worked specials were older. When I saw the friendly face of Hendrix I was relieved. You can tell from that first impression who is going to be easy going and who is going to be hell to work with. (Most of the time. It is not an exact science.)

Hendrix introduced herself as a part timer who had been with the company for nine years, and she had worked at the raceway for just as long. She had a rapport with all the people who worked at the strip and knew everyone's names and life stories.

Working at the raceway was different than working the "streets.". For sixteen hours I got to watch pretty cars go fast and all I did for medical care was clean out one cut. The raceway was a piece of heaven in Ryder, so of course it didn't take long for Ryder to screw this up.

Ryder has done a lot of stupid things but when they prevented Hendrix from working at the raceway and instead replaced her with a couple of napping newbies and shit went down? Yeah, Ryder lost their contract with the raceway and we lost a piece of heaven. Long live Hendrix. Some say if you go by the raceway you can still hear her cursing up Ryder.

36. The Man On His Way Out

It is the nature of Ryder EMS and to a lesser extent EMS in general to have a high turnover rate. At Ryder in the surrounding counties where we worked primary 911, the turnover rate was much lower than in The City with those who did backup 911 and transfers all day.

It was such that in The City if you made it to a year of working at Ryder then you were considered a "senior" EMT and quite possibly crazy for staying at Ryder for that long.

The turnover rate was not surprising for a multitude of reasons. Combine the low pay, long hours, back breaking work, rude patients, no sick days, being held hostage at work past your due off time, lack of job satisfaction, no educational opportunities and few chances for career advancement, and an indifferent and uncaring command staff and you've got perfect conditions for a six month turnover rate.

In fact it was a celebration anytime anyone managed to break free from Ryder's evil clutches. Even when people left to work a "harder" job at City EMS at least they were getting paid more, with better benefits, to work "real" EMS, and nary a transfer run in sight (which is something county services can't say).

For Outtie it was not to City or even another EMS service he was leaving Ryder to go to, it was to the glorious world of insurance that he went. The one day I worked with Outtie it seemed he talked about little else besides insurance and being a proper father figure to his girlfriend of three months' son.

Outtie left Ryder a few days after we worked together, but not before he bestowed upon me the affectionate nickname, "White Thunder." I felt it was suitable for me and appropriately awesome. Outtie was very much missed by me; awesome nicknames are hard to come by. But he is in a better place now, anywhere but Ryder EMS.

37. The Crush

Ryder EMS is an organization so strapped for employees that it forces its day shift workers to come in one extra day every two weeks. Being new my "mandatory overtime" day moved around every month. Eventually I settled into Mondays after four months of working.

It was on my mandatory shift that I first met and was partners with Nova. I had heard her name often, but had never seen her. This was mostly due to the fact that she was insane enough to work one of the 5am shifts and I would never get up that early unless fire was involved.

My first impression of Nova was that she was so tiny. I could not fathom how she was able to lift the stretcher into the truck. Even I struggled at my height of 5'8" sometimes. Now I am not a love at first sight sort of person, but I definitely decided she was cute and I wanted to get to know her better.

For me it was her personality which drew me in. She stumbled over her words. She was delightfully awkward. She had a great smile and I enjoyed being the cause of it regardless of how much I looked like a fool in the process. We had a lot in common and our conversations were easy and light.

I looked forward to every other Monday just so I could spend eight hours with her. However we were cursed as partners. The number of emergencies and weird ass runs with Nova far exceeded those I had with any other partner.

Picture us, both of us not exactly bulky females. Well dispatch seemed to send us the most combative psych patients, including a tiny twelve year old boy for whom it took seven people to restrain.

Goes to show it doesn't matter the size of the person, but the size of the fight of the person.

The same could be said for Nova. She was tiny, yes, but she was amazingly strong. After seeing her in action I was almost not surprised when she told me that she played rugby. However that led me to question, "Is she or isn't she?"

We've all played the game. We meet someone who we don't exactly think is straight. However we don't want to make baseless assumptions, so we do our best to collect "evidence" of potential gayness/homosexuality.

Nova at first glance seemed straight, and I didn't let myself even hope to think otherwise *until* she mentioned rugby. I know, I know stereotypes are bad and evil and aren't always true. However stereotypes exist for a reason and do tell a certain amount of the truth sometimes.

So we questioned each other. I was straight forward about my non-male attractions, except of course for my burgeoning attraction for the tiny blonde sitting next to me. Nova, on the other hand, did not want to openly say anything so I continued to collect my "evidence".

She played rugby in an all women's league. She used to own a motorcycle. She enjoyed camping and outdoor activities. With her personality she seemed like a tomboy and mentioned the faux hawk she had in college. All the evidence pointed a certain way, but I couldn't say for sure.

Not until she invited me to a party at her place. I didn't really know any people there. I tried to play it cool, but then I was introduced to Nova's roommate, and oh hey girlfriend.

I simultaneously felt good that I had finally had an answer and bereft that the girl I was crushing on for months had a serious girlfriend.

After the party when we worked together there was a certain amount of tension. It didn't feel right to flirt with someone who was taken, so instead I asked questions. When did she meet her girlfriend? How long have they been together? And oh hey you're gay?

These conversations informed me that Nova and her girlfriend were having some rough times. I wanted to capitalize on that fact, but my old fashioned values and total lack of game prevented our friendship from moving past the casual flirty stage.

And just like that it was over. Nova was switching to part time and wouldn't be working her mandatory shift with me anymore. She tried to pick up to work with me, but our schedules never came together.

Perhaps if I was more confident or braver or less moralistic we could have been more, but then again maybe it wasn't the right time. A year after Nova left, I saw her at a local club and we reconnected.

Maybe this time...

38. The Father Figure

When you work in a city which lies near some incredibly rural areas you meet some very intriguing people. Something interesting about Ryder EMS was that the people who worked in The City were very different that those in the outlying counties.

Rogers was by all accounts a country sort of guy, but in the same sentence as his love for hunting he would talk about Black Sabbath and his hippy days. He was open minded about the gay thing and treated me like a daughter.

Rogers and I only rode together a handful of times, since he worked mostly in the outer counties. Each time we worked together was a great time. He made jokes, offered paternal advice, and gave me rides home when mine fell through.

He was a tough, sweet man and one I personally would be honored to have as a father. He had a young girl he would do anything for and it was clear he absolutely adored her. He had that blend of toughness and gentleness that I think can only be found in the good men who have daughters. You probably know what I'm talking about.

39. The Whipped Boyfriend

Ryder is big enough to provide a plentiful dating pool, but small enough that everyone knows your business. There is something about being trapped in an ambulance for twelve hours at a time which seems to foster trew lurve among partners.

First the flirting, then the dating, then a relationship is started. I think I can speak for many when I say there is nothing more nauseating than enduring and witnessing the interactions of a relatively new couple.

The pet names, the use of "we" when I'm certain they mean "I", the excessive use of the word "babe", the constant touching, the fact that they are always together. It grates on our nerves and makes us want to isolate them in a bubble far far away on an island with no simian-like creatures to annoy.

Luckily in EMS we can do that by keeping the couples as partners. Unfortunately there might be circumstances that cause the two to be broken apart and cause each to be inflicted on a new partner.

It was with a very whipped boyfriend that I worked with one Friday. His girlfriend threw a hissy fit when they were split up and was only consoled by Whipped.

At first I thought I got the better end of the deal, riding with Whipped rather than her. But then I had to suffer hours listening to Whipped bitch, moan, and whine, when he wasn't on the phone talking to his "sweetie".

I guess theirs was trew lurve after all because they got engaged and married in less than seven months and had a baby five months later. I just hope that kid wasn't conceived in the back of an ambulance.

40. The Squirrel

We have a term we use in EMS, "squirrel". We use this term for anyone who seeks out runs (and trouble), particularly emergency runs. These are the types of people who will inform dispatch that they are closer to an emergency run than another unit and snatch the run.

Like nuts, these EMT squirrels will be possessive of their runs. Also they tend to be more excitable and gung-ho about their emergency runs. I'm not saying this is necessarily a bad thing, but I do not partake in these bushy-tailed activities. I do not want to generate more work for myself just for the experience or the adrenaline thrill. I happily let my emergency runs be taken by squirrels.

We have a number of squirrels at Ryder EMS, but I have only been partners with one bushy-tailed man, Squeaker. Squeaker wasn't a huge squirrel, but he would stop at any MVC, motor vehicle collision, we would pass, even if it was clear that no one was hurt. Ironically, Squeaker stopped at this one MVC with no one needing an ambulance and we missed out on an emergency run, all because we were too busy talking with the woman with back pain.

Even though he didn't mean to, Squeaker got his squirreling in later that day. I was two hours past my due off time and we were finally cleared to fuel our ambulance and go home. However right as we went under this overpass Squeaker heard a crash. I maintain I heard nothing, but he did and when we looked back we saw a semi had crashed into the low hanging overpass.

So we turned around, checked on the driver, and performed traffic control as best we could. The idiot truck driver, who couldn't read a clearance sign, was okay and we ended spending more time on traffic control than medical care. I made a new rule that day. Don't ride with a squirrel. They have the weirdest things happen to them.

41 and 42. The Twins

Identical twins are great, if you're a straight male looking for female twins who are okay with incest. However if you exist in the real world identical twins are just plain confusing.

By himself one of the Beanstalk twins was easily identifiable. The number of men who are 6'6" who work at Ryder number...well only two. Each twin towers above everyone else.

The Beanstalks are among that select breed that have been working at Ryder for years, long before I ever showed up. Of course at first when I saw the giant at work I thought he was the only one, but then I kept hearing these stories, about "the Beanstalk twins" and when they were described as taller than sin, I realized my giant was not alone.

The two in appearance were eerily similar particularly in uniform. Both were night walkers (worked night shift), often worked together and both messed around with dispatch endlessly. Despite their gargantuan strides they took their sweet time going anywhere. They each displayed an incredible amount of apathy for their jobs and both truly embodied all the night shift stereotypes.

That is where their similarities ended however. After working with each Beanstalk separately I was then able to tell them apart physically and by personality.

Johnny Beanstalk was considered the "funny, nice" one. Certainly Johnny was more personable than his twin, Robert. It became the running "fact" of Ryder: you want to work with Johnny and not Robert.

I found Robert to be the quieter of the two, but I was never able to see how Robert was "mean" compared to Johnny. Robert was a self-described ass and didn't have much patience for people who did not do things his way. Robert was not as friendly as his brother, but still easy to get along with in my opinion.

I also found their differences in general temperament, energy levels (Johnny has ADHD) and tastes in music. Johnny was a bouncy pop sort of guy and Robert an alternative rock kind of guy. Robert was quiet while Johnny kept a conversation going at the same time as he was doing one of a million things.

Still their similarities were striking. They both drummed on the steering wheel, had the same type of dry humor, and never planned on staying at Ryder EMS as long as they did. Then again they shared that last trait with nearly all who work at Ryder, including myself.

43. The Dwarf

I am a woman about average height, so statistically there a lot of women who are taller than me and shorter than me. However, there are short women and then there tiny miniature women.

I have to give those women their proper props because it is difficult to load the stretcher into the ambulance even at my height. I can't imagine the amount of upper body strength necessary for those miniscule women to do the same task.

Smurfette was a very tiny blonde woman and unlike My Crush (Chapter 37), she was very straight and had let us just say "ample tracts of land". Boobs, guys, she had big boobs.

Now I don't usually make it a habit of describing my coworkers' breasts, unlike my male coworkers, but for Smurfette these "assets" in combination with midget-like legs led to an amusing consequence in the ambulance.

In order to reach the gas and break pedals in the ambulance Smurfette was forced to move the seat all the way to the front. This of course put her rather large breasteses right flush against the steering wheel and the horn.

If only I had a dollar for every time her boobs honked that horn!

44. The Contradiction

When we talk about Democrats versus Republicans there is a clear divide there. It's simple to say who's for what and who's against a certain issue. Sometimes on certain issues we might stray from our chosen side, but typically we believe in a single set of values.

In this black and white world of political, social and economic views, Dane was a fucking rainbow. Dane remains one of the queerest people I have ever met and is not even a little gay. However he was deliciously flamboyant, and never denied that he was acting perhaps a little gay.

Dane didn't care that he represented himself that way, because he was a big supporter of gay rights and loved the gays. Additionally he was a very strong advocate of women's rights and animal rights.

Dane was also a gun shop owner. He was very passionate about knives and firearms and along with this, gun owners' rights. Additionally Dane was never shy about how he felt about Obama and his dissatisfaction with the man's policies.

Though he was not shy about sharing his opinions on social media, he never ever was impolite or mean to you if you had dissimilar views.

Dane had multiple tattoos, piercings, gauges in his ears, a crazy bushy mountain man beard, but never did any drugs, nor tasted a single drop of alcohol.

It was for sure always a good time working with him and when he moved from full time to part time to have more time for his gun shop; he was always willing to pick up a shift with you. Despite how confusing I found him to be he was always at headquarters with a smile and a hug. It's amazing how such a civil service as EMS can bring such different people together.

If it weren't for the crackdown on good employees Dane would still be working at Ryder EMS. They told him to get rid of his beard or be fired. The man, confident in his own self, decided to quit instead. Having talked to him since he quit I find him to be an even happier individual. It's amazing the effects of leaving Ryder can have on a person's overall happiness.

45. The Creep

It seems to be the case that there must be one particularly despised person in every division at Ryder EMS. In one of the surrounding counties this person was Elmer Fudd, who shared a bit in common with The Despised One (Chapter 25).

They acted like they knew more than they actually did, had questionable hygiene, and were at times creepy as fuck. A big difference for me was that I could handle The Despised One; I could not deal with Fudd.

I hated getting pulled to work outside The City because it turned me into a stupid person. I didn't know where anything was and didn't know the roads or hospitals well. They even had different paperwork. It was like the evil universe which parallels our own.

So when I was forced and believe me I was forced (I'm not proud of it, but I threw a tantrum and lay on the ground outside the time clock like a pouting toddler.) to work with Fudd, it was a double whammy of hate.

I had to endure Fudd while he explained the different paperwork like I was a moron barely capable of writing my own name. He did that a lot, explain things unnecessarily. Seriously, at one point he showed me where to write my name. See, I was guessing it was the box marked "Name", but he sure showed me…that it was the same box.

At least The Despised One never treated me like an idiot and only yammered on about his crazy ideas, not very bit of minutia that passed through his head.

I met his regular partner once. She was possibly even crazier than Fudd, but then again I guess she would have to be.

46. The Pre-Divorcee

I don't think that anyone who values their relationship should work in EMS. I cannot tell you just how many relationships I have seen fall apart due to the stresses of EMS. The only relationships I've seen have much success at Ryder have been between two EMS workers. I think this is because there is at least some understanding of the commitment required to this job.

However, even if both husband and wife work in EMS, if the relationship is on the rocks to begin with, this world will tear it asunder. This was the unfortunate case for the Shorts. Even though female Short worked at Ryder for six months I never partnered with her. I did work with male Short though one Saturday for the very brief time he worked part time at Ryder.

By all accounts Mr. Short seemed like a dedicated family man who loved his wife dearly. He seemed sweet and gentle and didn't feel threatened when I taught him a few things, unlike other men I have tried to help.

Mr. Short was sweet to me all day and when I told him I didn't have a ride home he offered to give me one. Mrs. Short had already finished her shift and picked us up. Their dynamic seemed friendly and comfortable. They seemed like a solid couple.

Two weeks later I heard they split up because Mrs. Short cheated on Mr. Short with a fellow Ryder EMS employee. I never saw Mr. Short again.

This EMS lifestyle really is best for us single folk.

47. The Medic Tamer

Paramedics are very much like lions. The best way to interact with them is from a distance or even better, with bars between you. The thing about medics is you never know when they're going to simply be indifferent to your existence or when they decide to dig in their claws and rip you to pieces.

Granted not all paramedics are like this. In fact I know a few medics who are perfectly wonderful to work with. However if I am given a choice between an EMT and a medic I will pick the EMT almost every time.

If you are medic with no personal skills you'll find yourself adrift in a sea of partners. The good medics might snag themselves a regular partner. But it takes a real lucky medic to get a regular partner who can deal with his or her personal dysfunctions.

The greatest of all Medic Tamers was one such EMT to a particularly dysfunctional medic. The six hours we worked together were largely uneventful. Mostly I was interested in learning how on a consistent basis she managed to work with a medic nicknamed, "Crazy Harry".

It was clearly apparent that the woman was patient in saint-like ways. She also was intelligent and I can't help but think this aided immensely, when Harry struggled to perform his job without freaking out.

I can't say that she necessarily enjoyed her time with Harry, but she managed to keep him in check, a rare feat for the excitable Harry.

It was with a general sense of sadness that I heard about her departure for greener pastures. With his tamer gone Harry took back to stalking the Sahara, seeking and searching for his next prey...I mean partner. Run fast my little EMTs, run fast and don't look back.

48. The Artsy Chick

It's true that we get all sorts working for Ryder EMS, but we do not have an abundance of creative folk. I don't know if that's because EMS has a more practical, conservative slant to it, or because this job ruins creativity.

Anyways, I was put with a newer person, Picasso, and I noticed she was different from most of my compatriots. She was very intelligent and had a college degree...also hipster glasses. Typically in EMS, the words "hippie" and "hipster" are said with a fierce sneer on one's face, but I thought the glasses were perfect for her, cute too.

Also weird was the fact that she was an artist. She went to school for art. I'm not sure what got her interested in the medical field, but when I met her she had her sights on either medical school or becoming a medical illustrator.

She was taking classes at the University for medical school pre-reqs when I met her, so I foresaw the inevitable of her switching from full time to part time, which I was sad about because she was cute.

What I didn't see coming was her decision to join City EMS. A lot of those City EMS guys are thick-skinned assholes and I couldn't envision Picasso working for them.

Of course this disappointed me even more because I would even see less of her. All of this before she had a chance to draw me Titanic style. Sigh. Mine is a life not graced with such culture.

49. The Younger Brother

There are some partners you get along with due to your amazing and palpable chemistry. And still there are others you enjoy because they remind you of someone you like.

In the cause of Lil'Bro, he reminded me of my younger brother. He had the same gangly figure and goofy personality. It was clear he was a dork, but of the self aware and cooler variety.

One time I caught (or rather I should say witnessed as no one was hiding or ashamed) Lil'Bro with another coworker, trading Pokémon on their Gameboy advances.

So even though Lil'Bro was a few years older than me, due to his relaxed nature and unabashed love of all things geekery, he felt much younger.

What else can I say? He cool.

50 and 51. The Special Ones

In an organization as large as Ryder EMS, certain groups form and cliques are created. In Ryder there was a big divide between those who worked primary 911 and those who worked primary transfers. A smaller divide existed between those who worked the streets and those who worked "specials".

All those fun things you can go to in a city: sporting events, concerts, music festivals, "fun" runs and races, even graduations and formal banquets; all of those need EMTs and medics to provide emergency medical assistance. These were our "specials".

Many of the "special" people worked at Ryder EMS part time and only worked specials. They never busted their butts getting run after run completed and they never ever got held past their due off time.

What they did was easy EMS. They would sit and watch the event, getting paid to do so, only really working if some medical mishap occurred. Most specials go by without a single emergency, so in essence it is easy money.

As a result of their popularity and a full timer's busy schedule, it was difficult to get even a chance to work a special. You could only pick up a special on your day off and even then there were hardly any open slots. Unless you were one of command's toadies you never got out of your normal shift on the streets to work a special. Someone's got to chuck granny and all her cousins!

One Sunday, I was partnered with someone who was getting off early so as we headed back to headquarters I prepared myself for the inevitable long wait for my next partner.

As my partner drove we saw one of our ALS units ahead waving us down. We stopped in the middle of the road and I was hastily told to get on the ALS truck. So as we blocked traffic the ALS truck kidnapped me.

I had literally no idea what was going on. I looked to my two new partners to clear up this mystery. I quickly recognized them both as "special" people.

Gopher was a young black EMT who had been at Ryder EMS for a while and undoubtedly knew his stuff. He also worked the streets, but mostly I saw him on his way to "specials".

Mother Theresa was an older medic in her mid fifties. She worked part time and all I knew about her prior to this day was that she was friendly.

From my partners I knew it was a special I was headed to, but what was it? The answer: a college volleyball tournament. I had to admit it was nice to be off the streets and able to relax at work for once.

I was additionally excited because this tournament was going to be at the giant coliseum that I hadn't had a chance to check out. One of the first things medic Mother Theresa let me do was wander around while they got themselves set up in the first aid area.

There is nothing like being in uniform and being somewhere where you are actually treated with respect. It makes a person actually want to help others. It was no wonder why the "special" people were generally happier than the rest of our miserable lot.

The only patient we had all day was an elderly woman who tripped and hit her lip. The rest of the time we sat, relaxed, and chatted. I learned about Mother Theresa's compassion for her grandkids and others. She struck me as an abnormal character to be working in EMS. When I count how many people who still feel as much compassion for others as the day they started working EMS, I would only need a couple of fingers. Truly she was an inspiration.

All in all it was a great experience and I only wish I was considered more "special".

52. The Semi-Regular Partner

I've had a lot of new people ask me how you get a regular partner. I usually laugh and let them know that it's not like picking a name out of a hat. You have to feel a mutual chemistry. With some like with Slate, you know you'll work out well even before you work together. And with others like Lenny, you eventually build a relationship based on time and complementation.

For some they've had just one regular partner and others have had many. Of course there are those poor unfortunate souls who never find a regular partner, drifting aimlessly amongst an ocean of personalities.

There was a period between Lenny leaving Ryder and Ryder allowing me to ride with Slate that I was adrift. I was like Goldilocks, continually shifting from the too hot bowl to the too cold bowl of porridge. It was never just right.

Then I found a fit in the place I didn't expect to find one: the female gender. Now I don't hate women. In fact I believe as a gay one I kind of think hating women would exclude me from the parties. That being said I do prefer male partners in general.

Men and I just know how to relate. They like women, so do I. I hate emotions. They usually aren't emotional. Most of them don't talk my ears off until they bleed and most aren't easily offended. There are few passive aggressive games and I don't feel like I have to watch what every word I say.

My next good partner, Awesome, had just gotten off maternity leave and was back on the streets. I hadn't spent much time talking to her before she had her baby. My only memories of her previously included her and her boyfriend being quite vociferous in their opinions on Ryder EMS.

I had no idea what to expect from Awesome, but I had convinced myself I wasn't going to have a good day. So I was confused when I found myself enjoying Awesome's company. We called for lift assist more than I might have with male partner, but otherwise Awesome was awesome to work with.

I could relax and not watch my every move. We didn't ever make it official, but we would fight to work with one another. This was at a time when dispatch was coming up with the daily partner assignments despite their lack of knowledge of how we worked together or even what we looked like. Due to this I never got to be with Awesome enough for us to bond as Regular Partners.

We even had an official song, despite Ryder's refusal to recognize our partnership. Like with many of my other partners, music was our escape and was the lifeblood of the truck.

Anyone remember that popular romance (cough porn cough) book, "25 Hues of Teal"? Of course you don't. I made up that title. But most of you know which popular book I'm alluding to. Well anyways I was resolute in my insistence about not reading this book.

Here Awesome was salivating over every page while I uncomfortably stood by. Eventually Awesome wore me down and I started reading that blasted book. Nothing like reading porn at work. And that's all I'm going to say on that.

I met Awesome's mom and babysat Awesome's kid. I was around when her boyfriend proposed and antagonized about daycare options. We became close and it was with a bit of reluctance when I was able to work with Slate finally. I miss working with her, especially now that she has left The City to work in a different division. While primary 911 is certainly not my bag, I wish her all the lovely trauma and full arrests she can handle.

53. The Absent Minded Professor

There are plenty of EMTs and even medics who shall we say aren't the brightest bulbs in the box. Even still there are the people that stand out for such amazing acts of not thinking. My favorite among these was Brainard, one of the sweetest men ever to work at Ryder EMS. Despite his temperament, after working with him once I never wanted to repeat the action ever again.

The problem with Brainard was that he never seemed to follow his thoughts through and had a bad habit of easily forgetting pretty much everything. I couldn't tell what was more terrifying, him driving or him performing patient care.

Brainard for whatever reason had a horrible habit of falling asleep wherever he was. Now if he was in the passenger's seat and we didn't have a patient I was okay with that. The problem was that he would fall asleep WHILE DRIVING. And not just once or twice, but consistently. I feel like a lot of atheists got in touch with their spiritual side (i.e. a lot of praying) whenever Brainard got behind the wheel.

When he wasn't falling asleep behind the wheel he was forgetting all sorts of things. One time we were going about our business when a weird voice came across the radio. "Um...someone left their radio here? At Subway? Um...Roger, copy?" I did my own amount of praying as I looked for our own portable radio. Nowhere to be found. I stared at Brainard. He looked back at me and said, "Huh. We were at Subway earlier." I stopped myself from smacking my forehead on the steering wheel and asked my partner, "Do you think you might have left our portable at Subway? I can't find it." To this Brainard replied, "Guess I did."

If it wasn't the portable radio it was our clipboard with the completed paperwork on it, or the keys to the ambulance or where the ER entrances were or where his name went on the paperwork. I'm surprised he even managed to remember his name.

Many of his coworkers tried to get him fired (as City EMS already had), but Ryder does not fire anyone who has a pulse (or who has a father on command staff). Nepotism! It's what for breakfast!

54. The Closeted Gay One

There are many reasons why one might decide to not disclose that they are gay. Maybe they are afraid of discrimination or even getting fired. Perhaps they fear being labeled just for their sexual preferences. Perhaps they feel that their private life should stay that way.

I may foster a lot of negative feelings towards Ryder, but with the exception of one asshole supply supervisor I never felt like I was discriminated against for being gay. In fact Ryder could almost be called gay friendly for all the gay folk it employs. I never felt like I had to lie about my preferences at work, and in fact Ryder was the first place I was completely open about my orientation.

So it was with this mindset that I could not understand Bachman. For the longest time I assumed he was straight. He was a quiet young man who was in the National Guard. I'll admit I didn't much think about him until I worked with him for the first time.

There was just something about him that I couldn't place. He never mentioned the g word and since contrary to popular belief gay people don't (just) talk about gay things I was left confused by him. Ultimately he was a decent partner, obviously new to the job, but definitely teachable. At the end of the day that was all that was important.

Then through indirect means Slate found out that Bachman was gay. Why didn't he say anything I wondered? So the next time I worked him I subtly and less subtly brought the gay topic into conversation, but Bachman refused to bite.

Even though Don't Ask Don't Tell had recently been repealed, I wondered if that was the reason for his silence. But who was I to talk? I want to join the Armed Forces as a doctor one day and I don't want to be singled out as a gay person.

Truly my efforts to gay bond with Bachman were fruitless. Then after just five minutes of talking with Slate and listening to Slate talk about his boyfriend, Bachman opened up about his. Guess I didn't have the right "equipment" to make Bachman spill his secret.

55. The New Yorker

Some people soak up so much of their personality and culture from the places they were raised. Usually this isn't so apparent until that person either interacts with "normal" people or moves away.

There are a lot of words I could use to describe my partner, Brooklyn. She was brash, opinionated, humorous, and had a love for rap and R&B music. But when you heard her talk and her accent all you could think was, "Nu Yarker".

I won't lie. I led a sheltered life growing up in the suburbs. There was some gang violence at my school, but they were the type of gang that named themselves the Purple Phantoms and dealt in prescription drugs.

Brooklyn told me how she had to keep a razor in her mouth at school, because she had to be prepared in case she got jumped on the way home. I asked how she managed not to cut her mouth all the pieces. She told me with a shrug, "you get used to it". My sheltered mind was blown away.

Simply put you did not mess with Brooklyn. One time she was called to help out another crew with a combative psych patient. When she got there she asked the patient what was going on. When the patient decided to answer by rather colorfully describing Brooklyn, the gauntlet was thrown.

Uncensored dramatic reenactment:

Patient: "I'm trying to get help! These fucktards took me!"

Brooklyn: "We're EMS! That's what we're doing, getting you help!"

P: "Fuck you Bitch! I'm from The City Mother Fucker!"

B: "I don't give a fuck! I'm from Brooklyn, New York. You ain't got fucking shit on me!"

That patient learned his lesson the hard way: You don't fuck with Brooklyn and you don't fuck with New York.

56. The Perfect Newbie

There are so very many things that new EMTs do which annoy the more experienced EMTs. In fact you can see my list of annoying newbie traits in Chapter 76. Pretty much every single new person, through no fault of their own, does these things when they start out, unless they have previous EMS experience (sometimes even then) or unless they are Superman.

I was partners with this guy, Superman, on his second day of working solo (without a preceptor). I expected him to be nervous or on the opposite end, a condescending know-it-all. He had a jock look to him, so I admit I wasn't expecting much from him.

Superman first surprised me with his calm, yet not arrogant attitude. He was more than receptive to my offer of answering any questions he might have had, but he didn't have nearly any. It was clear that Superman, despite his offensive lineman appearance, was very intelligent.

When I learned more about his background I found out that we had a lot in common. We both graduated from college with a B.S.

and both tried unsuccessfully to get into medical school. It was absolutely refreshing to share an ambulance with someone who didn't give me a blank face when I mentioned biochemistry or who knew what the MCAT is and the simple fact that you CANNOT PASS THE MCAT. (Nor can you fail it, so that's cool.)

Superman was a quick learner and never needed you to repeat something or explain it. The only newbie mishap wasn't even his fault. We were using a motorized stretcher and when he pushed the button to lift the stretcher, a stretcher strap which was caught underneath a wheel, broke in twain. He was so amusedly embarrassed at this "mistake" and I was grateful for it, because perfect is really found in the imperfections.

57. The Government Conspiracist

Verdad is one of those partners I have had that I experienced instant chemistry with. We understood each other, and had the same levels of introversion and dysfunction. In fact just after the first time of working together we planned to move to Montana together and get away from it all.

Briefly Verdad confused our chemistry to be romantic chemistry. I got to experience that awkward moment when you realize you're being asked out on a date, only seconds before the actual event happens. My response was a non-committal agreement and friending him on social media, which clearly stated my preferences were not for men.

Once we got over that little misunderstanding we were thick as thieves. Working with him was always a treat. He and I were so similar that for the most part I didn't feel like I was trudging through quicksand trying to relate to another person.

There was one major thing we disagreed on and that thing would be the government. Verdad was one of those libertarian folks who believe in free will minus rules and restrictions. They believe in the power of the people and the sovereignty of self.

As for me I love America and rules and even our stupid government despite its numerous flaws. I didn't realize how anti-government Verdad was until I mentioned that I wanted to join the military and he told me he doesn't trust anyone in the military, because of their loyalty to the government.

I never understood that part of Verdad. It seemed to him everything the government did bad or good was unnecessary. I listened with frustration that Verdad had no opinion on gay marriage simply because he felt the government shouldn't be involved in marriage. Be for or against it, but have an opinion! Verdad never voted in any election, but constantly complained about the officials elected.

Our friendship eventually withered away to texting and the occasional acknowledgement on social media. A part of this was due to his leaving The City to work in "Real" EMS, but interestingly enough the other reason had to do with a girl.

Read on gentle viewers for the whole story.

58. A Girl

This is the tale of an awkward love between my partner from the previous chapter, Verdad, and a girl. It twas a mighty and majestic courtship, which took place over the course of several months and ended in heartbreak.

I rode with A Girl once. I can say I never saw what Verdad saw in her. I mean how could he go from asking my fine ass out to asking another girl? My refusal to date him was supposed to make him pause before chasing after anyone else. (I kid. I kid.)

Initially when Verdad told me of his attraction to A Girl, I was extremely supportive. I knew that he was a bit gun-shy around girls, and A Girl was very friendly. I also knew that A Girl was extremely awkward and that Verdad was excellent at handling us awkward folk.

I took up my role as cheerleader and coach. I watched as Verdad and A Girl got closer and became fast friends. Increasingly I got the distinct pleasure of dealing with a love sick Verdad. It was almost amusing to see Verdad, who had an inherent distrust for all things government, place so much trust in A Girl's hands.

Apparently A Girl was not ready for Verdad's love. She had been burned in the past and had issues in forming relationships, which mirrored my own dysfunctions. As a result I found Verdad coming to me in his efforts to understand A Girl and her game of cat and mouse.

Verdad was patient, exceptionally patient, with A Girl. Two dates over the course of six months patient. It soon became somewhat apparent to me that A Girl simply was not ready to be in a relationship with anyone.

Of course by this time Verdad was stupidly and helplessly in love with this girl. He continued to try and then A Girl would pull away and get angry at Verdad for no good reason, or at least that's what it seemed like to Verdad.

I can't know for sure, but to me it seemed like A Girl wasn't used to having someone in love with her. She was scared of it, so she pulled away. When Verdad wouldn't give up and kept reminding her of this thing she was terrified of, she lashed out and got angry.

By the time Verdad was getting angry, I was furious with A Girl. I may have understood her side of things, but not enough to excuse her actions to my friend and the only one willing to fight for her. He loved her and she rejected him.

I was there for Verdad when he was angry and I joined him in that anger. But soon after he was forgiving A Girl, even though it was clear she hadn't really changed. Verdad knew I didn't think highly of A Girl anymore. It's true. I didn't. I don't appreciate those who hurt my friends.

Verdad and I disagreed on this and our friendship suffered. I have no idea where the two are I their "epic love" story, but at this point I don't care. I'm sure I'll be back for the sequel.

59. The Lesbian

Okay, I will admit that Ryder EMS was a very gay company, chock full of those pesky homosexuals. A good percentage of my partners in this book are gay. I am in fact of the gay persuasion, but some individuals you can't help but look at and have your brain scream, "GAY! GAY! That's a GAY!"

The first time I saw Butch I didn't even need to use my gaydar to label her. I'm pretty sure I could have figured out she was gay with my eyes closed. That's how much her gay shined out. Butch was simply a lesbian head to toe. It was many months before I had the opportunity to work with her, though I had become accustomed to her voice on the radio.

She had a slight southern accent and a distinct and loudly polite voice. To someone without much energy hearing her voice always made me cringe with its sunny exuberance.

Together we went on a long distance run three hours one way. Now you would think with the gay thing we would have something in common. Well we did have that in common, but absolutely nothing else.

She was a "married" (as married as gay people can be in a red state) country ex-marine. And I? Very much none of those things. We couldn't even agree on music, but I suppose we didn't even need music since Butch was a talker, of the non-stop variety.

Butch fit the physical description of a proper butch lesbian, a built tough woman with very short hair. I sadly will never be a proper butch lesbian and it rends my heart so.

But you know for all her butchness and ex-marine nature, she asked for a lot of help lifting patients regardless of whether help was necessary or not. Also she had a strange pride in having only worked in transfer EMS services. Most everyone outside of transfer EMS, considers transfer EMTs to be babysitters and not a part of "real" EMS. It's a black mark if you stay at any transfer service for too long. But Butch was proud, so all I can say is: Go Butch go!

60. The Constant Complainer

There are some facts that you can be certain of: the sun will rise in the morning, cockroaches will outlive us all, and if you spend any time with the man Jethro you will hear him bitch and moan about anything and everything to do with Ryder EMS.

Don't get me wrong. I love working with Jethro. Once you get past the complaints you find a very good and caring man. He is someone I worked with often when Slate and I were separated. We even approached semi-regular partner status.

Jethro helped me when I was buying a car and constantly supported my desires to become a doctor. But I think he had been working at Ryder for far too long. The poor treatment day in and day out had seeped into his very soul and made him bitter.

It didn't help that he was juggling a new wife, his first kid, paramedic school and becoming a volunteer firefighter, all while working fulltime at Ryder which could mean sixty hours a week. How can you be any sort of decent human being with that much on your plate?

I thought it was important for Jethro to vent his frustrations. He may have been even harsher than I was on Ryder EMS, but one, Ryder assuredly deserved it and two, I feared that if he didn't vent he would implode.

I've known Jethro since I first started and I have got to say I am proud of the man he is turning into. I met him as a paramedic student, who was just that, a paramedic student. He was not the extremely hard worker who champions for gay rights, simply because he got to know me and Slate as well as a couple of other gay folk. Jethro has over the course of my years at Ryder become a friend. So if by working with Jethro that meant I had to listen to him complain, I would gladly volunteer. In fact I will go buy a skirt and some pom poms and be his personal cheerleader.

61. The Secret Badass

I am a huge supporter of the veracity of first impressions. Many a time I have gotten poor first impressions from someone, while everyone else raves about this person. Fast forward a few months and the person has gotten themselves arrested. I trust my initial instincts, however they aren't infallible.

When I first met Brittany I thought that she was another girly girl who stumbled into EMS and would be shocked at how difficult this job truly was. I didn't think too much about her in the months after she joined Ryder, not really until we worked together.

She was still in her probationary period and I wasn't much in a teaching mood. As the day went on I realized that Brittany may have looked like a girly girl but she knew her stuff extremely well. She could lift and the questions she did ask were excellent.

Brittany was good, but it wasn't until we got a run for a "sick person" that she really shined. When we arrived on scene we learned that our patient was a recovering alcoholic who was going through withdrawal and actively seizing.

Now most new people would start freaking out and start acting stupid and spastic. Even some experienced people get dumb in emergencies. Amazingly Brittany kept her cool the entire time.

We had a beefy man thrashing all over the stretcher and Brittany kept calm. I was in awe. I've seen firefighters freak out over less. So my sincere apologies to Brittany. Some people are made for emergency medicine and she is certainly is one of them, girly girl looks and all.

62. The Immortal One

Most people I talked to about this book at work were cautiously optimistic for its publication. One person seemed to take an extreme invested interest in HIS chapter. He said he had never been in a book before and he wanted to make sure I didn't impugn his character.

He told me multiple stories I could use and even sent me one, which since I was so annoyed and frankly busy it took me a month to read. I mean God forbid I write what I want to write in my OWN DAMN BOOK.

I was sorely tempted to keep his real name in here so he would be able to easily find HIS chapter, but I don't think he'll want anyone to know this is about him.

Infamy, as I will call him and as he will forever rest in, is a decent fellow who sometimes forgets to think before he acts or talks. He once wore his EMT uniform into a bar to pick up a friend, had a drink, and ended up getting reported. He got a suspension for the act.

One day because he was in a "bad mood" (his words) he went after Slate and told him that gay shouldn't be allowed to give blood, because statistically gay men represent the largest percentage of people with AIDS. Statistically men make up the great majority of child abusers, but I wouldn't think to separate him from his young son (or I would, but just to make sure he didn't turn into a dick like his father). I wonder if it were to be true for black people in the U.S. if he would say the same. Black people are refused from giving blood thanks to statistics. I'm sure that would go over well.

He lost his driving for going thirty miles over the speed limit. He gave attitude to the nicest person to ever work at Ryder EMS. Heck he gave me attitude for not reading his story sooner. Because I spend my nights lying awake wondering what will I ever write about HIM.

But hey he wanted his story told so badly, so let's do it. After reading I'll admit it's a good story but it doesn't say much about Infamy, so you'll find the tale included in The New Yorker's Chapter 55, because this little idgit wanted to take all the glory and humor of this story for him, even though he didn't do jack shit.

You wanted immortality. Here you go. Here is your chapter. Now go fuck yourself for being so Goddamn annoying.

63. The Conservative

I support the right to your opinion. I may not agree with certain views, but I'm not going to try and force you to change the way you think. I've been through enough debates to learn that yelling louder does NOT change the hearts and minds of humankind.

Additionally I know that I do not know all, and people generally have reasons for why they think the way they do. My freshman roommate in college was conservative and we spent a few hours rationally discussing the issue of abortion. She didn't change my mind on the issue, but she make me realize wrong and right are relative and just because someone is decried as evil due to their views doesn't actually make them the next Hitler.

It was with this approach that I worked with Bible Thumper. He is perhaps the most conservative person I have worked with or at least the most outspoken conservative. But when you work in an ambulance you keep divisive topics to yourself, or at least try to.

At the very beginning of our shift I inadvertently angered Bible Thumper by poking fun of a fellow EMT. The EMT I was poking fun at didn't allow cursing in his truck nor taking God's name in vain. Telling an EMT not to curse is like forcing a fat person to eat nothing but green leafy things (which to be fair I too avoid like the plague). You might as well be wishing to win the lotto, your chances are better.

Bible Thumper considered this fellow EMT a saint and that I was wrong. I apologized and we moved on. We managed to bond over music if nothing else. I met his son and grumpy wife and tried to keep the charm going.

By the end of our shift we were on our way to becoming friends. We would be if it wasn't for the tactless network of the social media giant, Bookface.

Bookface will ruin relationships decades old, because everyone feels like they can say anything on their mind. They don't have to see the hurt they inflict and everyone is a bit more real when they are not forced to play nice and can hide behind a computer screen.

As a Christian I really don't mind all the God stuff my coworkers post on Bookface. A bit of it I enjoy. I have gotten used to the informed and uninformed opinions on our president and our local politicians. No one is attacking anyone specifically (perhaps except Obama) so I don't usually mind.

It really is only when Bible Thumper made a particularly vitriolic status on his Bookface that I lost my temper. He wasn't attacking me, but the way he wrote his opinion, immediately after telling anyone who didn't like it to defriend him caused me to do just that.

I would never let that distaste bleed into work, but I still think I'd rather not work with him ever again. I still treat Bible Thumper with kindness and respect, but I grind my teeth while I do so as I repeat the mantra, "Everyone is entitled to their opinion" ad nauseam until I convince myself that I believe it.

64. The Redneck Dipper

There are partners who you won't get along with and there are partners you have frustrating, insane days with and who you might secretly plot the murders of. And then there are the partners and shifts that are so unbearably uncomfortable that you start to think fondly of Spanish Inquisition torture techniques, for either your partner or yourself. You don't care anymore; you just want it to end.

Dipp and I had absolutely nothing in common. He wasn't exactly friendly or talkative. All I really knew about him before we worked together was that he ALWAYS had dip in his mouth and that he was missing a toe. The missing toe caused him to limp and the ever present dip made his voice over the radio sound like his tongue was in a constant state of semi-paralysis.

He worked night shift, but occasionally did a double shift and worked days. It was on the day portion of such a double that I was partnered with Dipp. I attempted to initiate conversation, but I didn't know how to talk to him. So silence engulfed the truck. Normally I would put music on to lessen the tension, but neither of us moved to turn the radio on. Plus I was weighing the endurability of twelve hours of silence versus twelve hours of country music.

The silence was oppressive and I only made it through the day by going to my happy place of Spanish torture. The lack of communication led to a lot of difficulties with lifting and moving patients and my back screamed in protest.

The only "bright" part of the day happened after we dropped off a patient at a nursing home. Fire doors were closed and one of the nurses said they were having an emergency. Then as we're getting ready to leave another nurse calls for our help. We rushed over and saw what was beyond the doors.

In the middle of the floor next to the nurse's station, a group of folk were doing CPR on what I could only assume was a resident.

Now there's something you should know about the division of Ryder EMS that works in The City. We don't get dispatched typically to "true" emergencies. I've worked a number of chest pain, shortness of air, and stroke runs, but never a major trauma scene, a gunshot wound (other than one with a BB gun), and never *ever* a full arrest.

A full arrest, when a person's heart stops, is the baptismal fount for "real" EMS, but for transfer EMTs, it is the Holy Grail. Many EMTs look forward to their first full arrest. Not me. I like my patients alive to begin with, so it was with a certain dread that I surveyed the scene before me.

Dipp seemed as stunned as me, so I focused on the basics. CPR was being performed, so I looked for an AED, an automatic external defibrillator, used to shock the heart and reset an ineffective rhythm. I asked the nurse for one, except they didn't have one. I looked at Dipp and said, "Get the AED," and Dipp did his very best to run/limp away to get the AED in our truck.

I tried to figure out what else we might need when Fire rolled in and got their AED attached. And just as Dipp was returning City EMS was there with all the equipment we didn't have on a BLS truck. It was with relief that I let the City EMS guys take over.

I had numerous Ryder EMTs tell me they would have snaked the full arrest from City EMS. I couldn't help but think that the patient would have died in their inexperienced hands. I didn't take the full arrest, but I did learn from watching how City EMS worked the man.

The experience additionally got me through the rest of my shift with Dipp. It was the closest I had ever gotten to working a full arrest and I had the memory of Dipp attempting to run happily lodged in my mind. Even on the worst shifts happiness can be found.

65 and 66. The Husband and Wife Team

Earlier I had planned to write out separate chapters for each of Team Marriage, the Smiths, but so much about why I liked them as partners and as people they hold in common, so though they are certainly two very distinct people they get to share a chapter. Just chock it up to Marriage (you know, legitimate marriage, not like this gay marriage thing I heard is spreading).

I first worked with John Smith. He was new and very open to learning. He was a giant of a man with a gentle heart and a personality to match his frame. John used to be in the military, but it seemed that all he kept from his time there was respect and manners.

John was always smiling and laughing. Though I had to work on Christmas Day and was very depressed about not getting to see my family, he kept me in good spirits. We sat on standby and talked about life. John reminded me of a dorky Dad, which he was, but one who could curse and complain about Ryder, all with a smile.

John and I were together when a call came over the radio for a boy who swallowed his "grill" and the crew who had gotten the run was confused about how a boy could possibly swallow a BBQ grill. For those of my gentle readers who are also confused, think bling not burgers.

John was amazing to work with, and when he told me his wife was starting at Ryder I was curious to see the type of person that John would settle down with.

I actually guided Jane Smith through her first three days at Ryder. I will admit I am not always patient with new people, but Jane seemed to take to my advice and even enjoyed my company.

Jane and John shared much in common, but there were key differences. Jane was quieter than her husband, though I think 95% of the world was quieter than John. Jane was more nervous about the job, but had (in my eyes) superior taste in music. The two both got frustrated, but Jane was more likely to be frustrated by the idiocy at Ryder EMS.

That was something, though inevitable, I hated witnessing. There is a period of time, usually around two months that new people are happy at Ryder. They're happy to have a job and the bright and shiny of being a REAL LIVE EMT (!) hasn't worn off.

After about two months that changes. They are tired from all the involuntarily worked overtime. They're cranky because at times the work is back-breaking and non-stop. They get sick of being treated terribly by dispatch, supervisors, and command. They start to realize there is little glory in working EMS in an inner city transfer service. The pay is pathetic, the hours long, and everyone around them can't stop bitching about how awful it is.

With the Smiths I watched as the attitudes gradually changed in each of them. The two got to work with one another, but that was it in terms of benefits. These parents of three struggled to find a way to make this job work out.

There is something about watching those new people you've helped become embittered by Ryder. You want to protect them, but you know that they have to make their own choices. All you can do is be there for them and commiserate.

I like to think they followed my example when they decided to move to night shift. They lasted about a month, before they did what the rest of us only dream of doing, quitting abruptly in the middle of a shift. I was sad to see such good people leave. Ryder simply doesn't know how to keep good people around. I've only worked here for as long as I've had, because clearly I am insane and have little to no self-worth as a human being.

67. The Passive Aggressive Bitch

There are only two people out of this hundred that I refuse to work with. The first, The Scary Bitch from Chapter 12, and the second was Passive Aggressive Bitch, or P.A.B. I may have not have had a regular partner at the time, but I got along with my rotating band of partners. Work still sucked, but at least it wasn't due to my coworkers. The Scary Bitch was long gone and I felt finally comfortable in my EMT position.

Then they hired P.A.B. and she came to the shift I shared with Slate, and things went downhill from there. Slate didn't realize it at the time, but we had actually met her before. We volunteered to help an EMT class with their practicals and this young woman was rude and unkind to us both.

However I am a fan of giving everyone a blank slate when I work with them for the first time. It doesn't matter what you've heard about someone. In the ambulance people change, for the better and for the worst.

Though I was not excited about being her partner, I tried. I swear I tried, but somehow P.A.B. had done research on me. She must have because I otherwise don't know how she so easily managed to piss me off so righteously and so quickly.

We took a 911 call from City EMS for back pain and generally I like to help my partner out by assisting and asking questions. Apparently this ticked P.A.B. off because she rather bitingly asked if I wanted to take over her run. No, I replied. I just wanted to help.

Of course P.A.B. didn't need or want my help. My method of conflict resolution with people I don't know is to avoid it, so I tried to let it go.

The rest of the day was spent trying to figure out a way to be friendly. Eventually we got to a point of reconciliation at the end of shift. I joked around and told P.A.B. it wasn't her, it was the fact that I didn't get along with my female partners as well as I did with my male partners. I was trying to help us get past our difficulties, but P.A.B. saw this statement differently.

A few days later I was confronted by The Majestic (Chapter 23) who told me she had heard from P.A.B. that I didn't like working with The Majestic, which was completely untrue. P.A.B. had decided to violate the unspoken rule of what happens in the truck stays in the truck and go to my female coworkers and shoot her mouth off, by saying I didn't like to work with them.

Was I angry? Oh completely, but that doesn't excuse my childish actions towards P.A.B. The next time we worked together I gave her the cold shoulder. It was silly and made both our jobs vastly uncomfortable, but it is amazing how anger can shield you from proper reasoning.

Once my anger abated the two of us tried again to reconcile. P.A.B. told me she didn't feel well, so I took a long distance run for her and let her drive. I was really trying to be a good person.

However once we dropped off our patient P.A.B. informed me she was either going home sick or she would make me do the rest of the runs for the night. I honestly informed her I'd rather not take all the runs for the rest of shift and that if she felt sick maybe it would be best for her to go home.

It was like I told her that her first child looked like a walrus. P.A.B. got angry at me simply because I wouldn't let her drive the rest of the night. I was already straining every fiber in me in my attempt to be nice. I had already done her a favor and had taken a nasty run off her hands. I wasn't looking to be a pushover for a girl I didn't even really like.

Our long drive back was quiet. P.A.B. was angry with me and I really didn't care that she was anymore. But then out of seemingly nowhere she started screaming at me. She insulted me. She told me that I hate her and screamed some more.

When I'm angry I lose my ability to reason, but when other people are angry I find I can be quite calm. Not raising my voice once, I try to address her "concerns" about my character and I repeat ad nauseam that I don't hate her. She seemed to never hear my words. It's true. I never hated her. We were awful partners and she could be unpleasant, but none of that caused me to hate her.

You know there is nothing like being screamed at while you're driving a death machine and navigating through traffic. I was very upset that I was getting yelled at, but I couldn't let it affect me.

We ended our night early and each explained to our supervisor our incompatibility. Though the words ran through my head and though my stellar reputation would allow for it, I never besmirched P.A.B. in front of the supervisor. I wouldn't risk her job simply because we were awful together. I don't know what P.A.B. said about me, but I wouldn't say anything bad about her.

I wish I could say we never worked together again. But Ryder EMS is an awful place and though there were other options she and I were placed together for an extremely uncomfortable and miserable three hours.

Honestly I was lucky to avoid her further. Slate got along with her and though he didn't approve of how P.A.B. exploded on me, he could appreciate her personality more than I could. No one could understand why I had such trouble with her. They told me that I can get along with anyone!

Not wanting to be awful I would say we were too much alike, which was true. We are both strong, stubborn as hell women who don't like being told what to do. I'm not as crazy as she is and I would never yell at my partner like she did, but sure, we're just too much alike.

When I left for night shift P.A.B. and Slate became regular partners for two and a half months, before he lost his patience with her and followed me to night shift. It did feel rather like justification for my feelings finally, and I'll admit it was great to be back with Slate.

Apparently things quickly went downhill for P.A.B. She was upset by Slate's "betrayal". At one point before Slate left, she even confronted me about Slate and though I had no inclination to be nice, I was and tried to ease her worries without giving her false hope.

When Slate left, P.A.B. rotated partners, until she left mid-shift one day and no one knew what had happened to her. Though numerous rumors abounded the facts were these: she had an outstanding bench warrant and was arrested. She was only in jail for three days, but Ryder EMS said she was a No Call No Show at work and promptly fired her.

I didn't want such a thing to happen to her, but I will admit it help spread the word not to be mean to me. Cause if you're mean to E.S.T., bad things happen…

68. The Gentle Giant

Most of the time you get to know your coworkers by seeing them around and hearing the rumors. Many of the people I ended up working with I got to know by talking with them around the time clock.

Paul Bunyan, however, was a man who rarely talked and thus it was difficult to get a read on him. I knew he was a giant of a man who seemed angry or at the very least stoic all the time. I knew he liked guns, but that was it. Any attempts to make conversation usually fell flat.

When I found myself playing partner musical chairs one day I found myself alone with Paul Bunyan. I didn't want to be with the giant, but it's not like the concept of free will exists at Ryder EMS. I did what I had to. I picked up our equipment and followed Paul Bunyan, eclipsed by his fearsome shadow.

Within seconds of actually interacting with Paul inside the ambulance, I found him to be quite friendly, funny and easy to get along with. I enjoyed my time with Paul so much that I would have picked him over scores of other potential partners.

So what does anyone remotely sane and awesome from Ryder EMS do? They leave. Shortly after we were partners Paul left not only The City, but The State, such was his desire to escape this human rights infringement of a company.

69. The Soccer Mom

You get all sorts of people working at Ryder EMS, but in the backup 911 transfer section of Ryder, you can find some general similarities shared amongst the EMTs.

The greater majority of these EMTs are in their twenties. Most are single or at least not married. It's the nature of EMS to attract these unattached single folk. There's no spouse to get angry with them when work forces them into a ridiculous amount of overtime. There are no children to make the EMT long for home, fearing their job is making them miss out on the milestones and important memories of childhood.

There are plenty of mothers and fathers who work at Ryder EMS, but none filled the bill of Soccer Mom so perfectly than Brandy. She had the physical appearance of a suburban mother, complete with "mom" hair. She looked like the person more at home behind the wheel of a minivan than an ambulance.

So when Brandy told me she hadn't worked in EMS for long I was not a bit surprised. Apparently her daughter worked as a paramedic for Ryder and when Brandy needed a job, her daughter talked her into becoming an EMT.

Brandy was one of those EMTs who hated EMS. She loathed the 911 calls we went on preferring the neat and tidy transfers. She didn't like to work at all and complained constantly about Ryder and EMS in general.

I wondered why she stayed. It was clear she didn't fit in or even like her job. I guess it kept her occupied now that her children were mostly grown, but then again so does knitting.

70. The Nameless

My memory is pretty decent. I could probably name you all 206 bones in the body. In the same vein I remember the name of every partner I have ever had at Ryder EMS...except for one.

It was a Sunday and I had no regular partner at the time so they were sticking me with anyone around. It was a very slutty time for me at Ryder. "She'll work with anyone!" No, I won't but I am very friendly and personable with new partners.

Anyways, on this Sunday I was partnered with this part timer. I could not tell you her name, but I can tell you all about her.

She was about 5'9", in her late thirties, early forties. She was a bit husky and had long curly black hair. This woman had been working at Ryder since the 90's though she went to part time after a few years. With her husband she worked at a surrounding county EMS service.

With me she was friendly and enjoyed our lazy Sunday and our abnormally lengthy standbys. I got off on time thanks to her and that's all I can say about her.

I have tried to figure out who this mystery person is, but no one has been able to help me out. I apologize to you, part time woman, and in memoriam of you I dedicate this chapter to all those EMS partners we have forgotten, their names washed clear from our minds by the excess hours, the blocks on the things we'd rather not remember, and the sheer volume of faces we see only once or twice. To you, the nameless, I dedicate this.

71. The Self Assured Fireman

All of the emergency services are tightly linked, but there is perhaps no connection closer than that between EMS and Fire. In many counties and towns EMS and Fire run out of the same station with many members cross trained to be both an EMT or Paramedic and a Firefighter.

In our city things were different. Our City EMS might standby and work out of fire stations in slow times, but other than that City EMS and City Fire were completely separate entities.

At Ryder EMS we employed many firefighters from smaller stations outside The City where they were mostly volunteer based. You could always tell among the new EMTs who were firemen. They walked with a clear swagger. They blustered around, dripping with testosterone. These old firefighters - new EMTs-felt entitled, because they had already seen everything and done everything, or so they thought.

They were cocky and didn't follow instructions, because they already knew it all. Scrappy was one such new EMT. Both Slate and I got the opportunity to break Scrappy into the world of no Fire EMS. We each painstakingly removed the layers of unwarranted confidence, false bravado, and ignorance.

I would like to think Slate and I were the reasons why Scrappy became such a great EMT, but I suppose that would be false bravado of my own. So I'll just say...no actually yes, we do take credit for him.

Perhaps the most telling way to determine a firefighter versus an EMT is how they drive an ambulance in an emergency situation with lights and sirens on. When Scrappy and I got an emergency run for shortness of air I felt myself transported to my happy place, because that was the only way that I could deal with the fact that I was going to die imminently.

Scrappy drove incredibly recklessly and pulled curves at speeds that had me reaching for my in-flight vomit bag. When I lightly suggested that he might want to slow down just a tad, he assured me. He told me not to worry; he was an expert at driving the fire truck code three.

Oh good, I thought, that's a comfort, as I clutched the sides of my seat in my AMBULANCE. Ambulance driving is and should be different from any other type of driving. Ambulances are generally top heavy and don't take fast curves well. They have a greater stopping distance which makes it all too easy to have hard stops which rack your teeth. And all this is not even considering what happens when you have your partner and a patient in the back.

Once we loaded our patient and Scrappy continued to drive like a maniac I became testy. Mostly because I was getting thrown around the back of the ambulance like a sack of flour, and not the expensive kind, but the cheap off brand kind. On a fire truck you don't have to worry about your unseatbelted partner who is trying to attempt patient care.

When the run was finished and before I started to count my bruises, I had a sit down with Scrappy. Despite his firefighter upbringing when I explained that safe is much better than fast (at least most of the time) and I told him that my life's aspiration was not to be a bouncy ball, he came to realize that perhaps being a firefighter didn't prepare him fully to be an EMT.

72. The Humble Firefighter

If you guys are actually reading this chronically and not picking out chapters at random, then you will remember my previous words on firefighters who become EMTs (hint, it's in the chapter right before this one). If you don't feel like reading back, then here is a synopsis: they are cocky, bad listening, know-it-alls filled to the brim with machismo.

Even if all firefighters are not as bad as I describe they all display the symptoms of the condition, every single one I have met, except one: Scooby.

I was with Scooby on his very first day. At the time it seemed like dispatch's favorite thing to do was to stick me with new people. I guess they felt that I would gently guide them as they forded the waters of Ryder EMS, that or they thought I would keep them from fucking up too badly.

When I heard I was with a brand new person and he introduced himself as an ex-firefighter I groaned internally. I was still working on deprogramming Scrappy (Chapter 71). I really didn't need another showboat.

I took a cleansing breath and tried to prepare myself to find new ways to get through to thick headed individuals. It took me a while to realize, so convinced was I that all firefighters couldn't listen to any criticism, that Scooby was different.

Scooby didn't act like he knew everything. In fact he admitted he didn't and asked a lot of good questions. He was never cocky and always listened to his patients and his partners.

He was new and at times dopey. He wasn't the quickest learner, but he at least was willing to learn and for that I give all the credit in the world to that ex-firefighter.

73. The Mini-Me

In a company as large as Ryder EMS you're likely to find at least a few souls which might resemble your own. No one in this company more closely physically and in some respects personally resembled me than Kinsey.

I joke and call her my mini-me, because though she is ten years older than me she is much much shorter. Both of us have shortly trimmed brown hair with glasses that make us look far smarter than we actually are. We both are very friendly and personable. We both don't drink and alas we both have caught the gay, likely from watching too many episodes of Golden Girls.

The first time riding with Kinsey was extremely queer (odd, not gay, though it certainly was) because we were just so similar. It was eerie. I wondered and still wonder if I would be a near replica of Kinsey in ten years.

The biggest difference between us is Kinsey is a much more open individual and is more assertive than my somewhat meek self. In fact Kinsey once made it her mission to turn me into someone who said "fuck you!" to the world and anyone standing in my way. On that, well, let's just say I'm a work in progress.

Kinsey is also more experienced in relationships than me, and has encouraged me to "get some!" Many times over. People say that. What exactly does "some" entail? Get you some dinner and fancy wine while engaging in intellectual discourse with the love of your life? Probably not.

A smaller difference between us is the fact that if we were to get in a physical altercation, an all out brawl, even I would put my money on Kinsey. She used to work security, but more terrifying is the fact that she used to work at a school for extremely difficult teenage girls. Yep. No challenge. Mini-me all the way.

74. The Overshare

I love road trips. I feel like the long hours spent in a vehicle together are often more bonding than the events you're traveling towards. I am a pro at getting through long driving trips and even relish them. There is a certain freedom in those trips when it's just you, your buds, and the wide open road.

At Ryder EMS every so often we'll get a very long distance run. We've been all over the country and even to that foreign land we call Canada. It is exceedingly difficult for anyone working full time to be put on one of these trips since they usually take several days.

But thanks to some luck and fast talking from Kinsey (Chapter 73) who was friends with the scheduler, we landed ourselves a lengthy trip to the exotic locale of Delaware. Three people were given the run, me, Kinsey, and a familiar face and part-timer, TMI Man.

Up until fairly recently TMI Man had worked full time at Ryder EMS and was one of Ryder's biggest opponents. TMI Man complained often and loudly, before he went to part time in order to take care of his new baby and paramedic class. Once part time TMI Man still complained, but now most of it happened over social media.

TMI Man and I already had a decent friendship before the trip. I was good friends with his fiancée and baby mama. With the combination of TMI Man and Kinsey this was looking to be a most excellent trip.

And it was. We had a blast. Our patient was a good sport and really friendly. He invited the three of us to feast with his family. The seafood was delectable and dessert scrumptious. Kinsey bought me a souvenir teddy bear and we started to make the long trip back. This is when our trip went from fun to strange.

It was midnight when we started back, no break to rest up. Ryder didn't exactly give us any money for anything but fuel. We were expected to drive through the night, which is fine. I've driven tired many times, but then a snow storm started, or really a blizzard.

TMI Man had made a deal that he would do all the patient care if he didn't have to drive, so Kinsey and I took turns driving on completely snow covered roads, up and down the mountains roads, going on no sleep in the early morning hours.

So how does one stay awake then? By discussing one of an EMT's favorite topics, sex. Now I will admit that I am not very open about my sexual experiences and I consider myself quite modest. However Kinsey and TMI Man were decidedly not at all shy in discussing their sexual preferences.

It started out so innocently. We went through all the women at Ryder and listed which we found attractive (or "bangable"). It was rather amusing to discover the secret attractions for our coworkers.

Then after we went through those fantasies, we then crossed over to what we enjoyed in bed and outside the bed. Although when I say "we" I mostly mean Kinsey and TMI Man. I was too busy driving and fighting down a blush.

I learned the most about TMI Man, much more than I had ever wanted to, and way more than I wanted to ever in any sort of reality, real and imagined, know about him and his girlfriend. I'm still traumatized by his words. I would love to scar you guys too, but I am a gentlelady (and an unintentional Puritan).

75. The Worst Day

Communication is absolutely essential in EMS. If you don't talk with your partner you risk the health of your patient, not to mention the health of you and your partner. However some people, no matter how hard you try are not capable of intelligent human communication with other humans.

I had the utter misfortune of being partnered with the very worst listener at Ryder EMS, name of Awful, on my worst day at Ryder. Now I have had a few absolutely horrendously terrible shifts at this job. I have cried. I have been injured. I have been vomited on, bled on, forced to endure verbal and physical abuse all with a smile.

I have been held hostage at work by Ryder for hours past my due off time because we were "too busy" with pre-scheduled transfers. I have gotten so much attitude from people outside and inside of Ryder EMS. I have been yelled at in front of all my coworkers, just because a certain captain didn't care for me. I have lost my driving privileges for the slightest of reasons. I have been treated like dirt and less than human. But none of this can beat the day I worked with Awful for the worst ever.

It was supposed to be my day off, but I was called to work an extra shift. I was promised to get off at 9pm. Of course I come in and there is no partner for me, so I am forced to wait. I wait an hour and call my supervisor. Can I go home, I ask. No, she says. I wait two more hours and call, can I go home? This was supposed to be my day off. No, she says.

I've been waiting three and a half hours for a partner and gradually losing my shit. I watch as a crew comes in with a truck with bed bugs. I watch the two men strip off their clothes and I ask about their run.

It was for an old lady who couldn't walk to go home. She was seen in the ER for knee pain, but the ER couldn't find anything. Apparently the patient and apartment she lived in were both crawling with bed bugs.

I was grateful I wasn't them. I hate bed bugs and well bugs in general. They give me the creeps.

I was planning on simply leaving as "sick" when I was told that they finally found me a partner. It wasn't home, but at least it was better than waiting or so I thought at the time.

The plan was this: the old lady that the crew had just taken home, now wanted to go to another ER, and City EMS didn't want to take the run. So instead of having the crew who had just taken the old lady do this run, they decided to give it to me.

Oh and we got to go out in the already infested bedbug truck. I was livid. Then I found out my partner was Awful, a wannabe medic who was known to me as an idiot with poor listening skills. The two of us got in the nasty truck and went to pick up this crabby old lady who of course lived up two flights of stairs and looked like something out of a horror movie.

I tried to explain what I wanted from Awful, but he completely ignored me and decided to do his own thing. Well that worked out really well for us both as our stair chair and the patient almost tipped over multiple times and I almost lost my footing and fell down an entire flight of stairs.

By the time we got the bed bug lady in our truck I was digging my nails into my hands in rage. We took the lady to a different ER than the one SHE JUST LEFT and when we got there Awful just left.

He left me in the bed bug truck with this crazy lady to go "explain" the situation to the triage ER nurse. All Awful had to do was drive the truck. It was MY job to explain. I waited for twenty minutes on Awful. My anger had progressed to wishing destruction on everyone in my path.

Finally, once we were free from dropping the bedbug lady off we were free to go back to headquarters to decontaminate ourselves and the truck. I was hoping they would let me go home. I could decon at my home far away from this horrible place. Awful heard my desire to go home and decided to call dispatch and talk on behalf of me, though I told him not to. So of course he ended up getting me in trouble with command staff.

A Major came over to inform me that not only was I not going home, but I had to strip to my underclothes and wait until my uniform had gone through the dryer. (Excessive heat is something which kills bed bugs.)

I am modest. There was no way I was going to parade around in a see through gown and my underwear in front of everyone. I contemplated bringing up sexual harassment when the Major offered me an empty conference room to wait in while my uniform heated.

So for an hour I waited half naked without even my phone to entertain me. My anger had dissolved into the desire to burst out crying, which I did in that empty conference room.

By the time I was dressed again there was a single hour before 9pm. I pleaded to anyone to please let me go home. What could I manage in an hour? Haha no, they said. They would get that one last run out of me and Awful.

We got a non-bed bug ridden truck and made our way to the run. I carefully explained to Awful that I wanted to do this run as quickly as humanly possible.

Awful agreed and then decided to stop for food at a busy fast food place. It took twenty minutes to get his food, which he just HAD to have before we did this run. Not only that, but when we got on scene he spent another ten minutes chatting with another Ryder crew.

At this point I was at a level of anger where I usually black out, so I don't remember anything else until Awful and I were at fuel, past 9pm and much later than we should have been. I'm calling and trying to get in touch with my roommate so she can pick me up.

Awful overheard my conversation and decided to, without any prompting, call the supervisor and beg for a ride for me. I didn't get along with this supervisor at the time and understandably he was miffed. He had other, more important things to worry about than how I got home.

So now, once I had a ride all setup already, Awful had gotten the supervisor pissed at me, command pissed at me, and dispatch pissed at me and I hadn't even said a single word to any of them.

I was as close to quitting that day as I have ever been while at Ryder EMS. I still don't know how I managed to not strangle Awful or spontaneously combust from just how angry I got.

Bad days are going to be bad days, but they are infinitely worse with a bad partner.

I never worked with Awful again. He left for City EMS after he got his paramedic, but he came back and as Ryder does promoted the idiot to supervisor. Because of course they would.

76. The New Person

It is amazing how much disdain there was in Ryder EMS for new people. So many people acted like they were given a death sentence when they were given a newbie EMT.

EMTs don't tend to be new for long. I generally give an EMT two months before they stop fucking up all the time. Granted this is an average. Some EMTs stop acting like chickens with their heads cut off in just a week, but some don't get there…well ever.

There was a period when after Slate and I had been at Ryder for over a year when we got seven new people on our shift over the course of four months, so we couldn't escape them. I have a lot of patience for new people, but when I switched to night shift I about kissed the scheduler in gratitude. That was until I found out about the two new people on my new shift.

Anyways during this period of perpetual, agonizing newness Slate and I came up with a list of things that new people stereotypically do which bug us to no end. Since one of my partners acted new for four months and most of our list applied to her I thought I would include the Best Hits Version of that list.

Newbies are easily spotted by the ever present stethoscope around their neck, seen even while clocking in, and the bling on their uniform usually name tags and American flags. An old EMT knows that you don't want all your patients to know your name, especially the psych ones and the assholes.

Newbies are obsessed with taking vital signs yet cannot take a blood pressure in a moving truck.

Newbies love to freak out. In fact they do it so much I swear they practice in the bathroom mirror before they come into work.

They will freak out about psych patients who will of course kill them manically, even the sad, depressed ones, with the trauma scissors you carry on your pants or your pen! Don't let a psych patient handle your pen! They'll stab you in the eye! Or so the newbies think. Sad to say, the great majority of my psych runs are perfectly boring.

Newbies freak out in emergency situations and turn into the clumsiest, most babbling nincompoops you've ever met. They don't understand that there are different levels of emergency and that rushing before thinking could end up with the deaths of you, your partner and your patient.

Newbies even freak out if the blood pressure deviates even slightly from 120/80. Once I heard my partner asking if his patient normally had high blood pressure. Curious, I called back, "What's his BP?" My partner replied, his bling reflecting in the sunlight, "142/90, do you think we should go code three?" My internal response was something like, 'No, but he should probably lay off the cheeseburgers and French fries.' But instead I gently explained that 142/90 is a perfectly stable BP and I would not worry unless it was forty points higher.

New people are also terrible drivers, absolutely horrendous. This makes perfect sense when you work at a company that doesn't actually train you to drive an ambulance. Depending on their personality new people either drive like they are insane or like a four foot ninety-five year old woman.

Newbies also want to follow the GPS exactly to the point mile and then get upset when the exact point mile puts them in the middle of a bridge. The response is always the same, "The GPS told me to go here!" No. The GPS didn't tell you, it advised the rough approximation of your destination. The GPS does not think, so it does not recognize it is in the wrong place. However my new human partners don't have the excuse of not being able to think and should at least know to keep their eyes open for signs or address numbers.

The worst thing about newbies is that they don't watch what they say and get shitty with the wrong people. For instance you DO NOT get shitty with your supervisor…unless they *really* deserve it. Also do not give crap to the ER triage nurses. They have excellent memories and the ability to keep you and your increasingly annoying back pain patient waiting for thirty minutes just to get told to drop them off in the waiting room.

As a general rule I advise all my new people to be kind to nurses. Our job sucks. Their job sucks more. They may get paid more, but then again they have to spend more time with the soul sucking patients, deal with more of their crap than we do, and deal with bossy, ignorant doctors.

The last thing I tell my newbies, in the hopes it will be the one thing they remember, is to bring band-aids. I say this because they will run the stretcher into my shins, roll it over my feet, fling seatbelts at my face, throw me all over the ambulance and crush my hands under stretchers, patients, stair chairs, and bed rails. And I've got to say I'm sick of stocking my own band-aids.

77. The Unlucky One

Poor poor Two-Leaf Clover. I have had my share of unfortunate mishaps and of course they spread through the gossip network like a misshapen, grossly misrepresented fire, because ultimately make believe is always more interesting than simple facts.

Two-Leaf, he had the misfortune of doing something that was legitimately gossip worthy without any need for embellishment. I suppose for me it was good that this one unlucky event happened to him, because otherwise there isn't very much to write when it comes to Two-Leaf.

I worked with him a few times when he was new. He was bright, respectful, and quiet. It was nice for once to have a partner who talked less than I did. Riding with Two-Leaf was peaceful, a nice change from the crazy world of working EMS in a city.

Two-Leaf was by all accounts a great partner and human being, so of course the universe has a way of ruining that. Despite how it happened, it was not all Two-Leaf's fault.

It was a busy day and someone wasn't paying much attention to the partner assignments, because they put Two-Leaf with another new person. Had Two-Leaf been placed with a more experienced EMT, he might have known his ambulance clearance was 9 feet.

And had he been with a more senior tech he might have been told the correct ambulance entrance at the nursing home Two-Leaf transported to. However Two-Leaf was not that lucky.

I came back to headquarters that night and found everyone all atwitter. Apparently someone had sheared off the entire light bar off the top of one of the ambulances.

Eight months later they still won't let Two-Leaf drive.

78. The Unapologetic Douche-nozzle

I was raised to believe in the values of hard work, that at the end of the day all that mattered was that you always tried your hardest. Perhaps no one over the age of forty would believe that young people with work ethic still exist, but we do.

However Douche Canoe isn't one of them. I personally have a strong distaste for anyone who uses their charm or wiles to decrease their workload. Douche Canoe oozed with charm; he was just about dripping with the stuff.

He was lazy and only average at his job, but due to his sweet talking nature no one noticed or cared. When we would pick up patients from the floor of the hospital, he would find a seat in the nurses' station and flirt with all the nurses while I did all the work. He even cheekily answered the nurses' phones to many of their shock and displeasure.

So it was with a fierce glee that I found someone not charmed by Douche Canoe. We were taking this middle aged woman from the ER to her home and she did NOT like Douche Canoe. He of course came into the room sweet talking and this, admittedly psychotic woman started accusing him of treating ME badly.

She started going off on him and men in general and how they all treat women badly. When Douche Canoe asked me to stick up for him I couldn't because I was biting my cheek to keep from busting out laughing.

Apparently Douche Canoe was so hurt by this woman's rejection and my refusal to stand up for him, that he gave me and my patient the worst ride I have ever had in an ambulance. And it wasn't like Douche Canoe was a bad driver, he was actually decent at that. No. He did it on purpose.

There are some times with certain patients that I will break my safe over fast rule, but ONLY when both partners agree. I entered into no such agreement with Douche Canoe Suffice it to say, I was livid.

There are moments when we aren't as friendly as we could be, moments when we display characteristics of douchery. Well, Douche Canoe was that moment.

Like many before him his time at Ryder EMS was brief and I for one celebrated his departure.

79. The Other Company Man

In a city of any reasonable size, you're going to have multiple ambulance companies. In our city we had four major companies. First, in their minds at least, was City EMS who only did 911 runs. They never sullied their hands with transfers or dialysis runs, and hogged all the trauma and good emergencies.

Next biggest was my company, the wondiferous Ryder EMS. It had the major contracts with the hospitals to do transfers and a contract to do backup 911 for City EMS. The company does a lot of business and generates a tidy sum which then gets...well I don't know where the money goes because we get paid three dollars less to the hour than City EMS.

The smallest company had about two ambulances and had a contract with maybe one hospital. They don't do much, and are easily made fun of, but then I learned they get paid more to do less work and I started crying.

Our biggest rival is the other for profit company, ERI. ERI has a national presence, but not as much in The City. Also they've had their share of scandals: Medicare fraud, striking members, and losing a major 911 contract in a surrounding area because their units didn't have the drugs they needed.

My partner for the day was from ERI and you could tell his time there had not been good to him. Why he thought Ryder would be any better, I don't know, but he lasted longer than I thought possible for anyone with any sense of dignity, three months. He can now be found working for the smallest company in The City. I don't know who is better off, but I don't think it's me.

80. The Smoker

Despite the fact that EMS is a medical field and we are confronted with the consequences almost daily, a metric shit ton of people smoke in EMS and Ryder is certainly no exception.

Ryder, as a company, hates smokers. You lose out on financial benefits if you smoke (and you can't lie about it, because they test your blood). Ryder can't stand all the downtime crews use while smoking.

I am a non-smoker. Always have, maybe always will be. So I don't know how to commiserate with a smoker's plight. I get impatient with my chimney stack partners. One in particular, Marbolo, would smoke a cigarette before a run, after every single run, sometimes more than one cigarette, and between runs. When you have around ten runs a shift, that's a ton of cigarettes.

EMS is crazy for cigarettes. At any time of day and I mean *any* time you can find at least one person outside of headquarters smoking. Sometimes it's crew members, sometimes supervisors, and definitely dispatch. I hardly see any command staff smoking there, but I think that's just because they have a better hiding spot.

The very first box of cigarettes I have purchased was for a partner. And I won't lie. I felt cool buying those death sticks. Often I lament the fact that I don't smoke because it seems like the best gossip happens in smoking circles.

But then I watched as my partners smoked in all conditions: rain, extreme hot/cold, tornadoes and I felt much cooler inside my temperature controlled ambulance.

I doubt this smoking problem in EMS will be solved at any time in the future. Fact is EMS is a stressful job and EMTs and medics all search for easy ways to take the edge. At the very least smoking is a better method for this than high risk illegal midnight drag racing (based on a true story).

81. The Soulmate

I have been with over a hundred partners at the writing of this chapter at Ryder EMS and not a single one can approach Slate as being the perfect partner for me. He was my second regular partner, but if Ryder hadn't figured out constant and new ways to keep us apart we would have been regular partners from our first day.

First we couldn't work together because we were both new. But by the time we were past our probationary period I had lost my driving and due to his age Slate couldn't drive either.

We weren't able to work together until we had been working at Ryder for seven months. Even so, that lasted just a month before I lost my driving again (this time not having anything to do with my driving, but with something that I will keep secret about, because it was a single moment of stupidity and I have suffered enough).

Then the next time we were able to work together was after we had been working at Ryder for over a year and had become "senior techs". The new problem was the seven different new people on our shift. Since new people can't work together we were constantly split up, infuriatingly so.

Even when Slate turned twenty one and got his driving privileges, the new people kept us separated. Then I switched to night shift to take a class, and Slate stayed on days.

Truly ours was a tale of two soulmates torn asunder by time and circumstance. It was not until we had been working at Ryder for a year and a half that Slate followed me to nights and we FINALLY actually got to enjoy being regular partners. There aren't a lot of new people or people in general on night shift and now that we're both drivers if one of us screws up, we don't have to get split.

Slate and I have been friends since EMT class and inseparable (as much as Ryder says). However unlike with Lenny, the dating rumors between Slate and I were very short lived.

Slate is not a blindingly obvious gay man, but he sure doesn't shy away from the subject or letting his coworkers know where he stands. I did not even know until at the end of our first week of class he talked about how much he liked Britney Spears. Not very many straight men brag about their love for female pop icons.

It was refreshing being partners with Slate for numerous reasons. The greatest was that I was always comfortable in the truck with him. He knew my family drama, my hopes and dreams, and created a safe space for my rants.

Slate knew that I say mean things about everything and everyone, and he didn't judge me for it. Most of Ryder thought I was the nice, friendly one and Slate was the snarky, mean one. But I was much meaner than people thought and Slate was far kinder than anyone gave him credit for.

Slate was a wonderful and incredibly giving friend. He's done so much for me that I haven't even asked for, and I've seen him be the same way with his other close friends.

Slate has been with me at my worst and at my best. Slate endured me for two months while I freaked out about the MCAT and studied non-stop. Slate was instrumental in the writing of this book. He would be reading a book and I'd bother him by asking him about a certain partner or read off something I had written to get his thoughts.

Though it is less obvious than with Lenny, my strengths and weaknesses complimented Slate's. While I am a pushover, Slate doesn't let himself or I get pushed around. While I am calm in emergencies situations, Slate tends to get a bit frantic. Slate has the upper body strength that I still don't posses and I have a good ear for the radio and dispatch calling when Slate is lost in a book.

It is amazing just how smoothly things go with Slate. We have a flow and a pattern to how we do each run, but even still we do our best to communicate because we know we're not mind readers. Everything about work is easier when I'm with Slate.

For the first year at Ryder, Slate had some issues with how he presented himself. He is at times a bitchy gay man and though he doesn't generally mean to give attitude, that's what people hear. I had a supervisor come to me in my first month of work to tell me, I had to "talk with my friend" about how he talks with supervisors. The conversation with Slate was a decidedly awkward one, but instead of getting defensive Slate was curious. Slate was quick to come to an understanding with the supervisor and now the two are best buds.

Slate's "attitude" also had him getting into trouble with nurses. Up until I worked with him I listened as he told me about this bitchy nurse or this asshole CNA. When I started to work with him I did start to notice nurses being rude and mean to Slate but in part it was how Slate worded things and the tone of his voice.

Now when Slate gives attitude it is no misconception or mistake. I helped Slate with his presentation and in turn he saved my life.

When I am on scene I have a tendency to be extremely focused on my patient and patient care. I don't see my surroundings and that has been not a good thing. I first was told about this character flaw when I didn't notice a gun on this one family member's belt.

With Slate I have missed so much that he has seen. There was the crowbar under the bed, the handgun on the table, and oh how about the knife in this guy's hand! We eventually developed an innocuous code word for "weapon" so Slate can subtly point out the things that I miss. To properly demonstrate how oblivious to such things I am, once on scene on a City EMS run Slate took my flashlight and used it to point out the weapon and I still didn't understand what he was doing or even that he was trying to catch my attention.

It was with Slate that I went on my creepiest run. We picked up a schizophrenic male and took him back to his group home in a tiny tiny speck of a rural town. The facility looked like an old converted church and had no sign. Outside the facility men aimlessly wandered about even at eleven at night.

Once we got our patient inside we saw about thirty men, all with different psych issues, mostly schizophrenia. What made it great was not the guy screaming in the hallway or the way the men were way too close to me (despite the short hair they saw what scores of elderly folk did not – that I actually am a woman), or the stains on the floors and walls, but the fact that there was no security or even a nurse or any staff to be found.

Eventually the men who seemed all too comfortable in my personal space led us to the kitchen where the only staff member for the entire facility had locked herself in. I don't blame her for a second.

I've been to a lot of psych institutions, but none has been as true to a horror movie as this "institution" was. Luckily I had Slate to help fend off the worst of them. Thinking about that place still gives me the chills.

Slate was also my soulmate because he cared about keeping a clean, organized truck even more than I did. Every truck we worked in was left much cleaner than before we took it out. One lazy Sunday Slate and I even climbed up on the truck to clean the light bars. Our stretchers, every part of it to the handles, to the various hooks, and frame got thoroughly wiped down at least once per shift. Neither of us can think clearly when there is a mess.

Additionally something we agreed on nearly completely was music. Even though I banned country music in my truck with Lenny, he found that if he played it when I was busy with a patient in the back that I objected less.

Slate didn't hate country, but he'd rather listen to my eclectic mix of music from my iPod or the pop, rock, and indie radio stations I chose to listen to. I cannot simply stress enough the important of musical compatibility.

This is not to say we agreed on absolutely everything. In fact I have a tendency to (infuriatingly) force Slate to look at an issue from multiple perspectives. Then again other times I say, "Fuck Dispatch/Command/Captain Dickbag" as well.

Slate got hungry for something every hour while I never ate. He and I both got grumpy when we're tired and I know he was ready for me to stop spouting off random MCAT factoids.

I endured his rants and him mine. He was sometimes able to follow the scattered thoughts of my brain and I tried not to actively cringe when Slate was driving and rushing us to fuel or headquarters.

Slate's been there since the beginning and he'll always be my number one. He's my best bro in and outside of work. And I sincerely hope that he remains my partner until I, he, or we leave this company how we came into it, together.

82. My First Medic

For a period of a year at Ryder EMS I had achieved the near impossible. I had never ridden with a paramedic. Paramedics are terrible at keeping regular partners so usually they will stick any poor sap they can with them. I only avoided working with one for as long as I did because I couldn't drive the ambulance.

I wanted my first time with a paramedic to be special, like any other first time. I knew several medics, and got along with them. I didn't want to work with them because I didn't want have my inexperience in ALS to ruin my relationships with them.

My selection process was stringent, but in the end I choose to ride with Alpha, a part time medic I did a run with once. It was an ALS run so they sent me and Lenny a medic to do the run with. I had heard of Alpha and his antics, but this was our first interaction. We transported our patient to a cath lab so that they could remove a clot in one of the coronary arteries of his heart.

When we dropped off the patient I thought Alpha would want us to leave right away. He had volunteered his time off for this run, so I thought he would want to rush out. But when Alpha found out Lenny and I had never seen an angioplasty performed he stayed. We watched the procedure and Alpha explained to us what was happening as the surgeon worked.

A friendly medic interested in answering my silly questions? Yes please! Alpha was very amenable about picking up a shift together.

We picked up on a Sunday. I was nervous about the emergencies and failing my medic, so I thought a lazy Sunday would be perfect for my first ALS shift.

While the BLS trucks did run after run, we stayed on standby. We didn't do a single run for the first six hours of our shift. Alpha even got bored enough that he asked dispatch to change our standby to a busier one.

A chunk of our downtime was spent in the company of another BLS crew. It was in their company that I learned just how incestuous Ryder EMS was. The men listed all the women they had slept with at Ryder and proudly showed off the pictures on their phones of their various conquests. They ranked the women and intimately described certain physical attributes of the women. I swear I was blushing blood red the entire time.

Alpha and I only got one emergency run and I got my first experience at attempting to give a smooth code 3 ride while the medic tried to start an IV. Because he is awesome Alpha got the IV in. It seems like a miracle to me anytime a medic can get an IV in when we're moving.

All in all it was the perfect first time. My only disappointment is that I don't get to work with Alpha more often.

83. The Boyfriend

I guess there are some men who love women so much that they love ALL women. They feel like they are so suave and so fine that no lady can possibly refuse them. Of all the men I have been partners with at Ryder, Man Whore was the worst to work with. He was cute and friendly and charming. He was a huge player and for a time really loved to flirt with me. But hey a handsome guy flirting with you? What's wrong with that? This gay lady will tell you.

Men who think they can change the lady loving ways of lesbians simply with the irresistible draw of their machismo confuse me. Lesbians are into women. Pretty much the definition.

Man Whore wanted me. Why? I don't know, because every straight man wants to bag a gay lady? Because apparently I'm so hott that Man Whore didn't see my sexual orientation, just my lithe body? Fuck if I know. But he was scarily persistent.

I explained to him the gay thing many times over, and in the same sentence of him telling me he understood he would offer me sexual favors. My problem was that I was too polite, too nice. I should have told him to fuck off from the beginning, but I didn't want to be mean. Screw that. Especially with what happened one night after working together.

We were talking and walking to our cars. We got to his car and all of a sudden his face is way too close to mine and he's kissing me. I didn't know WHAT to do. I was startled into silence. His gross wet lips pressing into mine, and when he pulled away he SMILED.

I love straight men, I do. I get along with them far better than I do with most women. But straight men, a little advice, if you want to keep those weird ball things you have between your legs then DO NOT KISS YOUR GAY LADY FRIENDS.

84. The Asshole

Don't get me wrong. There were plenty of assholes who worked at Ryder EMS. I didn't work with them all though. Most of the people I have worked with may be flawed, but were not truly assholes. Also "asshole" tends to be used hand in hand with "medic" and the number of medics I have ridden with I can put on one hand. Asshat was not a medic however, but he should have been just for the way he treated others.

My first experience with Asshat was early on in my EMS career when I was working a double. I was exhausted and was on my last run. We went to a residence to pick up a guy for dialysis. The guy we were sent to already had a reputation for being shall we say...difficult. Difficult in the sense that he groped any female EMT he could get his hands on. He was also tragically overweight, but the Big Boy, bariatric, stretcher wouldn't fit past his doorway. Since I was partnered with another girl, I called for lift assist to help us out.

I asked for help and I got Asshat. When he and his partner got there he immediately insulted us and proceeded to talk down to us. Asshat tried to tell us how to move the patient and made fun of our patient in such a way that even I felt for that fat prick.

Now I am known for being extremely polite in person, but I was tired and extremely irritated, so I went off on Asshat. I, in no uncertain terms, told Asshat that this was MY patient and I would be making the final decisions. I also asked would he ever so kindly stop treating me and my partner like we were idiots. He's the only coworker I have ever directly confronted like that. Asshat was stunned and relented.

For a year this was the only interaction I had with Asshat. Then I switched over to night shift and ended up on the same shift as Asshat.

Asshat was one of those EMTs who had been at Ryder for a lifetime (a few years) and it had turned him hard and extremely cynical. Thus it was no surprise that he had a regular truck, but no regular partner.

On my very first day of night shift I was partnered with Asshat. I cringed inside for many reasons. The first was that I was worried that he would remember me and my attitude towards him. Luckily not everyone has the elephant memory I do and he had no idea who I was.

I decided I would do my best to not antagonize Asshat and get along. I wasn't very hopeful for the night when Asshat introduced me to "the rules of HIS truck". I stayed friendly and polite, even in the face of his condescension, even when he interrogated me, by asking several questions about my experience in EMS. He claimed the questions were so he knew what he was getting into.

The rest of night lurched on as Asshat wasn't content to let me be. He would play some 90's or classic rock song and put me on the spot asking me for a song title and band name. I played well enough that he lightened up.

In fact after the first unpleasant night together, he warmed up considerably. He joked around and made fun of me. He was still being an asshole, but at least he was being playful about it.

One night together I informed him of his "asshole" reputation. Asshat knew he had the reputation, but couldn't understand why. In light of our improving relationship I didn't feel like providing a list of examples.

I stand by my opinion of Asshat, but at least once he gets to know you he is an asshole who cares. One night we had a pick up out of an ER to go to the psych floor of the VA. Unfortunately the ER we picked out of was unaccustomed to dealing with violent psych patients and had not one, but two old, decrepit security guards. Our patient, a schizophrenic veteran, did not want to go, refused to leave, and threatened all of us. He was young enough and big enough that manhandling him was no option.

Psych patients don't usually scare me, but this veteran was terrifying. Asshat saw my hesitance and put himself between me and the patient. Now Asshat isn't a large man and this vet towered over him, but I knew Asshat would protect me. Forty minutes after we arrived we managed to coax the guy onto the stretcher. Asshat got into the back with the vet and with clammy and shaky hands I drove to the VA and called for security to meet us.

I listened as the vet screamed and talked of death and killing. My ears certainly perked up when he told us he was going to slit our throats. Fortunately for everyone we got him to VA with no incidences.

After the run when I was trying to calm myself down, Asshat told me that if I was ever scared by a patient he would step in and take the run.

So I stand by my word that Asshat is an asshole, but he's one I would want by my side, or preferably in front of me, as a human shield.

85. The Seminary Student

We get all sorts of people, from all sorts of walks of life, but very few individuals go from the religious life to EMS (unless they're a Baptist preacher, we get a lot of those). It's not surprising. Who would go from the relative peace of religious studies to the dirty, hectic, soul crushing world of emergency medicine?

Apparently Emerson would. He came to The City to go to a major and popular conservative seminary. Emerson was a student for a few years before dropping out. I am still unsure whether it was due to money issues or theological ones.

Somehow Emerson found himself working at Ryder EMS not long after I started. I remember seeing him come to work night shift with his semi-regular partner. Emerson seemed rather shy and quiet, but certainly friendly.

When I first started on night shift and I was put with Emerson, I was pleased (especially since it met I didn't have to deal with Asshat, Chapter 84). Emerson was easy going, good at his job, and intelligent. He exposed me to new and interesting music, though I could never join him in his appreciation of talk radio.

I knew the reputation of the seminary he attended, as one of hard-right wing values. Emerson never brought up politics or social issues, so in wanting to keep the peace neither did I.

It was fascinating to see how EMS had hardened even such a gentle soul as Emerson. He would make biting comments about his fellow man that an intelligent seminary student would never even allow himself to think. It just goes to prove, it doesn't matter how hard you fight it or who you were before. EMS will change the way you see people.

As much as I didn't want to stir the pot I found I couldn't help myself any longer. My curiosity had to be sated. The two of us went on a long distance run to the next city in another state. After we dropped off our patient we decided to grab some food.

So it was in a fast food joint that I finally unleashed my question on Emerson.

"Emerson, how do you feel about the gays?"

It was a question in which I had an obvious personal stake, you know me being a big 'mo and all.

Emerson seemed to consider the question for a minute. I prepared myself for the worst. Then Emerson spoke intelligently on the subject.

He told me that he saw gay people who engaged in homosexual sex as sinners, and said he also felt the same way of those who had premarital sex. But then he explained that since we are all sinners, who was he to judge anyone else for their actions? Only God could do that.

I may have not agreed with Emerson's views but I most certainly could respect his thinking. He didn't quote bible passages at me or condemn me to hell.

Perhaps if more Christians were like Emerson, we would have more Christians.

86. The Normal One

I thought in writing this book I could prove that everyone has that spark in them that makes them special or interesting. I tried so hard to come up with such a trait for my partner, Smith, but I could not think of a single thing.

She was perfectly normal. She wasn't boring and she was pleasant to ride with, but she was standard issue. She worked part time at a county EMS service, but never bragged about it. She didn't like working for Ryder EMS, but that was a very popular opinion among those who worked for Ryder. She was good at her job. She...She...

I've got nothing! She was normal. I guess there's always got to be one...

87 and 88. The Devil And Angel On My Shoulder

When I first started on night shift there were these two new guys on my shift: Maverick and Athos. Those two represented very different ends of the moral spectrum.

Maverick was an eight year veteran sergeant of the Marine Corps. His claim to fame was that he had been arrested for public intoxication on four different continents. To Maverick rules were to serve as a guideline and not a strict doctrine to obey. Maverick was the one to take me to my first strip club and teach me which were good strip clubs and which were too sketchy.

Athos, on the other hand, was a wide-eyed, considerate young man. He was homeschooled and was a true God-loving and people-loving Christian. He married young and was a fan of magic tricks. Athos felt strongly about his faith, even tattooing the Fruit of the Spirit from Galatians on his upper arm.

The differences didn't stop there. Maverick was at first quiet in that creepy serial killer kind of way whereas Athos was personable and very chatty. Maverick had not a single care as to what people thought of him. Athos was very worried about the image he presented.

Both had their strengths and weaknesses and both were great partners. For a while I would go out with one and then the other the next night and they kept switching it up. As such with their very different viewpoints I began to perceive them as the devil and angel on my shoulders. It was uncanny how well they fit those roles.

Then something happened to make me strongly question this assignment.

Athos and I were transporting a patient from a nursing home that we were familiar with. She told us she needed to tell us a story. You could tell by how she said the words that there was not going to be a happy ending to this story.

We both got in the patient compartment to listen. Our patient told us she witnessed two nurses' aides abusing her roommate. It was a startling story. Once we dropped off the patient we called our supervisor and he, I'll say it, dropped the ball on this case. I had never been in this situation before and wasn't sure how to proceed, and with the supervisor lending no help I was confused and very conflicted.

Athos seemed genuinely more concerned for how I was taking it than for our patient or her roommate. I wondered why he wasn't more upset or enraged. During this confusing time I told Maverick what had happened. He immediately suggested going straight to the police. When I was struck by inaction Maverick kept bugging me to do the right thing.

Maverick was now the angel and Athos the devil. Action battling apathy. Before I brought up the issue to a 3rd supervisor (the 2nd had treated the issue even worse than the first), in my frustration and guilt I said out loud, why couldn't we forget that it happened? Maverick hit me right in the gut with his next words. He said, "I'm disappointed in you. I expected better from you."

Internally I was furious. Who was Maverick to be disappointed in me? Once that wave of rage passed I realized he was right to be disappointed. The situation may have been complicated and my supervisors may have done nothing but that shouldn't have stopped me from doing something for my patient and her roommate.

The world is not black and white. Sometimes your angel is sweeping the messy things under the rug and your devil is burning the rug to make sure you don't forget the messy things.

In our attempts to be "good" people sometimes we fall short. But if we fall hopefully you too have a friend like Maverick to remind you of what is right, even if it's not easy.

89. The Anal Medic

I had been meaning to work with another medic since My First Medic (Chapter 82), and found my chance on New Year's Day. I figured that the combination of a holiday and working with a medic would lead to a nice, slow day.

The medic I worked with that day, Da Anal One (!) or Dao, I was already somewhat familiar with. She and her husband were both medics at Ryder EMS and had established themselves quite differently.

Lady Dao, my medic, was very exact and had little tolerance for stupidity. She looked and sometimes acted like a strict librarian. One time my first regular partner, Lenny, was forced to ride with her. Apparently it was a very bad day for both of them. Lenny came back pale faced and told me how she yelled at him all day. So while I was a bit more intelligent than Lenny I wasn't sure how the day would go. I was still very inexperienced when it came to ALS equipment.

Well I lucked out for the first half of our shift, because we got nary a run. Dao took a nap and I tried to fight the boredom. Eventually things picked up and I proved to be at least competent.

We actually shared a lot in common, so it wasn't difficult to get along with Dao.

The only event that perhaps went a step above my own level of rigorous rule obeying happened during a hospital to hospital transfer. We were outside the patient's new room. Dao headed in to get the bed in place so we could move the patient over. I went to help Dao and she immediately reprimanded me and told me to stay with the patient. I wasn't that scared to leave my super stable patient for a minute outside his room by himself. But my personal rule for dealing with medics goes, unless your patient is going to suffer, the paramedic is always right (or at least you pretend they are). Day goes by so much better when you adhere to that rule.

90. The Hyperactive Chatterbox

I have been with partners who talk a lot. As it is I am not the most loquacious and it is real easy for a partner to dominate our conversation. The majority of these partners have been female as stereotypically women talk more than men. However the most annoyingly chatty partner I have ever had was a young black man.

From the second I walked into the garage I could hear Sonic yammering away about what God only knows. When I learned Sonic was to be my partner for the night I cringed. I had gotten used to the peace and quiet of working night shift and here was Sonic ready to fuck that up.

I do my best to be a good listener to both my patients and my partners, but I had to tune Sonic out or risk going (more) crazy and choking him until he passed out. I tried to focus on the music on the radio or even bring the outside stillness within, but with each word Sonic was chipping away at my calm.

Sonic reminded me of one of those yappy, tiny dogs whose only worth is to look "cute" and to bite the ankles of visitors. I'm sure there were people who would like Sonic as himself, but I was not ever one of them.

I managed to catch some luck, because we were brought back to headquarters to split up.

It was the longest hour of my life, and probably ranks for the longest hour in human existence. I still shudder when I think of that time.

91. The Part Time Medic

We have a number of part time medics who have worked for Ryder EMS for decades upon decades, since the advent of Ryder EMS. They work full time at other EMS services and fill up their free time with extra hours at Ryder. Some work for City EMS, but most work for outside county services, outside the umbrella of The City.

J.T. had been with Ryder pretty much since it started. No one knew him by his odd last name, just by "J.T." J.T. was extremely specific about the hours he worked when he worked at Ryder. He worked for only eight hours in the early morning hours of the night.

J.T. didn't come to Ryder to work. He came to sleep. In fact J.T. always became quite grumpy when forced to work more than he wanted to. He enjoyed working with me. I want to say because I'm not an idiot, but sadly that wasn't the reason.

I was "lucky". In two shifts of working with him we only had one non-emergency run. We got to sleep through the night when I was his partner. Other partners of his weren't so lucky.

J.T. was always really kind to me, so I was surprised when I heard from two friends who worked with him. They said he treated them awfully and refused to do any work, leaving it to his EMT and student medic.

Perhaps another rule to working with medics, especially night shift medics – they don't like to work and anything you can do to lessen their load is appreciated and with some medics, expected.

92. The Sleeper Agent

People who have worked on night shift for awhile, unless they are writing a book or enduring a partner who is writing a book, all possess the fabulous skill of sleeping in odd places. They are lulled to sleep by the roar of a diesel engine and the darkness of a well hidden choice of standby.

I wish I could fall asleep in the ambulance, but mostly my unscheduled sleeping happens at inopportune times like when a holocaust survivor told his story at my school or my college graduation. Yes I know; I'm horrible. Mine is a curse.

No one in all of Ryder EMS was better at sleeping than Narco. She was the champion of dead-like sleeping. I would say she was one of the undead, but I've seen zombies livelier than Narco when it's naptime.

Every single time we got a standby she would head to the back of the truck to lie on the bench seat. On the last standby we sat in a dark parking lot for two hours. Apparently it was long enough for Narco to achieve a comatose state.

When we cleared for fuel I yelled back that we were moving. Nothing. I drove down bumpy roads and all the way to fuel. I looked back and nothing. I had to pause for a second to make sure she was breathing.

I fueled the unit and emptied the trash and cleared us for headquarters. At this point I had to wonder if anything would wake her up. I drove all the way back to headquarters and ended our shift. I thought she would at least wake up when we got off work. Apparently not.

I even opened the doors right next to her head to grab our equipment, and still not a stir. She might still be on that bench seat if I hadn't needed the pager on her belt. Though I'm sure it's one of my gentle reader's fantasies, I did not feel like groping my dozing partner in the middle of a busy headquarters just to get a pager.

When she finally woke up she was completely disoriented and I'm not even sure she knew her full name.

The only logical assumption from this is that Narco MUST be a sleeper agent for THE GOVERNMENT who immediately feels the need to go into a state of false death when a radio says the word, "standby". Truly it's the only logical assumption.

93. The Complete Opposite

The saying is "opposites attract" right? Well I would like to challenge that statement. I mean you might lust after a busty babe if you are not in fact busty or a babe, but at the end of the day if you have nothing in common, you have nothing. How can you relate to someone when you don't have a single thing to talk about?

This is the problem I encountered with Yang. She was a loud mouthed, no filter having, boy crazy country girl from a small town. She was essentially everything I was not. I didn't know how to talk to her, so mostly I listened.

I don't think you can find two people at Ryder more different than me and Yang. She grew up in a small town where it was considered scandalous when she got a bob haircut and went to prom with a black boy. She had never met a gay person before and knew everyone in her tiny rural country town and they all knew her. I, on the other hand, went to a large public high school in the northeast where our dress code was not to show up naked.

But Yang was friendly enough that it wasn't bad working with her except for one thing. I hate country music. Growing up I was never exposed to the stuff and never learned to love it. I'm pretty easy going, but too much country and I go insane. Unfortunately Yang loved country. I swear by the end of the shift I was willing to stick anything sharp or damaging into my ears, just to not have to hear one more person whine or croon about beer, women, or his love for his pickup truck/tractor.

Physics may tell me that when I put two opposite charges next to each other they are inevitably drawn to each other, but when it comes to Yang I'm pretty sure no matter how opposite we are we will break the laws of physics and each of us will carefully walk away in two very different directions.

94. The Infuriating Medic

In a period of just two weeks I was stuck with this medic, Paragod, on three separate occasions and he steadily bothered me until I couldn't stand the sight of him at work.

The first time I got pulled to work 911 in an outlying county. It was a slow night and we only had one run for a fall out of a nursing home. This medic had decided it wasn't necessary to board and collar this patient, contrary to my own belief. As we're loading the patient into the truck the medic decided he didn't feel like taking the run, and gave the patient to me. I can handle unexpected changes like that, but I sure don't appreciate them when you could give advance warning, but choose not to.

I should have known what sort of medic he was then. The second and third time we worked together we worked in The City. I watched as he pawned off an ALS run to a BLS crew. He clearly was allergic to work.

What caused me to become furious was his backseat driving and his desire to aggravate me on purpose, because it was fun to him. No matter how well I drove he poked fun and seemed to hate red lights. He wasn't happy unless I ran every red light, emergency or not.

The teasing was unending and after a while I found myself getting flustered and making mistakes. Of course the more mistakes I made, the more Paragod teased me, and the more flustered I would get. By the time we were on our last run I was at my breaking point.

It was a non-emergent run from one hospital to another. Paragod hated GPSes, so mine wasn't up. In fact Paragod's favorite torture device was to quiz me mercilessly on how to get to different places. He was never happy with my choices and always made me come up with three additional routes. I know my way around The City pretty well, but I often set my GPS up, just in case I am so tired I lose focus or forget a turn.

Well in this instance I could have used my GPS, because somehow between hospitals I became convinced we were going to hospital A, when we were actually going to hospital B. Of course Paragod noticed when I made a wrong turn and so convinced was I that I was correct that I did something I usually don't and snapped at him.

Of course a few seconds later I realized he was right, but I couldn't tell him that! I rerouted to hospital B, and swallowed my pride. After we dropped off the patient I finally admitted to my error. Paragod was so cheeky about it I wanted to kick him quite squarely in his giblets, but I am professional, so I kept all my actions internal.

Ugh. Paramedics.

95. The Hottie

I am sad to inform you guys that there is a lack of truly hot women at Ryder EMS. Plenty of attractive women, but it seems like the hot women avoid such a masculine and male-dominated profession as EMS.

However there are a few stereotypically gorgeous women. Humpsalot, (who chose her own name. I wanted to go with something benign like Morrowland), was one such woman. She was blonde, thin, with a beautifully sculpted face and body. It seemed all of Ryder EMS was discussing her when she first started precepting.

Many of us, including myself, were disappointed that she was going to be working on night shift. I was working day shift at the time and felt I was never going to be given a chance to work with her.

Then I moved to nights, but even still she and I worked on different shifts. It wasn't likely that I would get to work with her. Not impossible though and I found her waiting on a partner one night and my wish was granted.

I tried not to drool as I introduced myself. I hardly knew what to say. Luckily she easily filled the silences with her chatter. Despite her appearance, she showed herself to be extremely easy going, a self proclaimed hippie.

I learned a lot about her that night as my mouth remained not functioning. She broke my heart when she told me about her husband and son. Even though my dreams of u-hauling it to Massachusetts were dashed, she was so much fun to be around, the hurt was greatly diminished.

Humpsalot was a spitfire, a bundle of nonstop energy and emotion. She didn't shy away from those expletives EMTs love and was joyfully optimistic without ever being completely unrealistic. She was a real treat to work with, plus I can't say I did not enjoy the envious looks sent my way when I worked with her.

96. The Obsessive Compulsive One

I will fully admit to my own compulsive traits. I like to keep my trucks neat, organized, and clean and I spaz out when things get too messy or disorganized. Monk brought that to a new level.

It was a long time before Monk and I were ever partners, despite our paths continually crossing. I got to know the woman's regular truck long before I got to know the woman.

Monk was one of the few individuals at Ryder EMS who had a regular truck, and the only night shifter to have one. Med unit 224 was well known since it was the only ambulance in the fleet covered in labels.

Each label was hand written and lovingly made. Personally I enjoyed taking out 224 because it calmed my inner control freak. Others did not feel similarly. Once all the labels were ripped off and I still don't know if EMTs or someone working in supply did the deed.

Before we worked together Monk and I bonded over our mutual desire to bring a semblance of order to the chaotic world that is

EMS. Monk cared about Ryder EMS, certainly more than I did, and had ideas and energy, but nowhere to properly express either.

Our single night together was pleasantly spent working through some of these ideas. Monk finally was given a chance to work on these ideas as the new head of supply. I was personally grateful for the regime change. The old supply captain and I didn't exactly see eye to eye. We disagreed on one key issue. He hated gay people and I "choose" to be gay.

At the time Monk became supply captain, Ryder EMS was going through a lot of changes. A new head boss guy was brought in and he was a breed of boss I was not used to encountering. He not only listened to our concerns and complaints he did something about them. He actually started to hold command accountable for their actions and jobs.

Monk's assignment to head of supply in many ways reflected the new regime. She wanted to standardize equipment and trucks, act in cost conscious ways, and she cared about morale and making the company better.

I could tell that she struggled at her new position. She was constantly at work and was never given the help she truly needed to make her division great. But that seemed to be in line with the motto for the new regime: work harder now, in the hopes that it will be better in the future (they never could tell us when, just "in the future".). Well Monk worked harder and found her better future...at City EMS.

97. The Ancient Medic

I have mentioned previously when I wrote about The Buddha (Chapter 24) that people who have been at this company for decades seem to adopt an attitude where nothing seems to get to them. They are unflappable; you can't flap them. They are a gently shifting reed in the wind.

Reed was a full time medic who had been with Ryder EMS since the 80's, 1980's, not 1880's that is. I never even had a conversation with her until I switched to the same night shift as her, and even then she kept to herself.

Previous to working with Reed, I had heard nothing but good words about her as a person and medic. She may have been a cat lady, but everyone protected her. She was Nana, everyone's grandma. She was sweet and soft spoken with hugs given out rarely, but when you got one you were transported to a land of freshly baked cookies and homemade meals and everything was okay.

I never shared but a few words with her until I got to work with her one night. The thing which bugs me about working with a medic (or one of the things) is that unless you have a big emergency, your job is to drive your medic, haul your medic's stuff, and if you have a female medic do all the heavy lifting when it comes to patients. I feel like my IQ drops 30 points when I work with medics. My brawn is much more favored over my brains.

Reed was good to work with. You didn't know where you stood with her and she was hard to read, but it seemed as long as you listened and didn't possess too overbearing of a personality you were fine with her.

Mostly Reed, along with nearly every other night shifter I have worked with, wanted to sleep. So I drove us to standbys and I let her nap while I studied.

She was the first medic I actually considered becoming their regular partner, and ignoring the part time medics, she is the only medic I would be happy to work with.

But then Slate came to my shift, and all considerations to become Reed's partner went out the window. Bros before Hoes.

98. The Slut

Now as an educated woman I know I should not be slut-shaming and yay for sex-positivity and on and on and on. However if you cannot keep it in your pants until you are off work and you get caught, I have to judge you a little, especially if you have sex in an ambulance.

For those not as familiar with the medical field of late then you will likely not know what I am talking about when I mention MRSA, VRE, and C.diff. These three are abbreviations for three different types of infections. These particular infections are common in hospitals and nursing homes and can be treated with antibiotics. However some strains of these infections are resistant to several different types of antibiotics and are life threatening.

A good number of our patients that we transport, especially since as a transfer company the majority of our patients have been in and out of hospitals and nursing homes, have at least one of the three mentioned infections. Combine that with the fact that most EMTs and medics won't clean their stretchers or seats off unless bodily fluids get on them, and you have a dirty, disgusting truck.

Now imagine having sex on that. Who would do that!?! There was one coworker of mine that not only had a habit of having sex in the back of the ambulance, but it seemed the guy she was doing the horizontal limbo with changed every couple weeks. All of that seemed very unsanitary to me and like an issue for the CDC.

Excuse me while I shudder in revulsion.

99. The Fat Medic

I don't like to work in the outlying counties where we do primarily 911. I'm neither an adrenaline junkie nor a squirrel (for my definition of squirrel check out Chapter 40). I have worked enough emergencies that I know what to do, but I'd rather not work them. Truly EMS is not where I belong, but it is what pays the bills for now.

Unfortunately I am not always given a choice as to where I get to work. I work mostly in The City of transfers, but occasionally will get pulled out to work 911.

They sent me out thirty minutes away to work in this itty bitty town where I'm pretty sure no one lives. My partner, Couch, was an experienced and incidentally overweight medic.

Now for a short word on fat EMS workers: I have noticed in my time here that the average EMS worker for City EMS is a hundred pounds heavier than Ryder in The City. One medic for City EMS I saw try to run, before he stopped, red faced and sent his partner to grab him the portable oxygen canister...for himself.

A combination of too much sitting around and diets consisting of a lot of fast food led to the problems of fat EMTs and medics. It also probably doesn't help that it's hard to find any time to exercise with the little time we are left with after our sixty hour work weeks.

It was an issue clearly Couch struggled with. She informed me that she never ran anywhere, even in an emergency. She repeated the common EMS phrase, "It's not my emergency. It's theirs." What ran through my head was that I didn't think she could even run if she tried.

The two of us lucked out in terms of our standby location. We got a firehouse complete with bathrooms, fridge, microwave, TV with cable, internet and beds. After looking briefly at the worn, discolored mattresses we both decided to relax in the recliners instead.

Pretty soon Couch was asleep and if you have ever seen a very overweight person sleep in a chair then you're probably familiar with the phenomena of horrifically loud snoring. As her neck got swallowed up and her head fell into her chest I worried that her airway would be compromised and I would have stick a tube down her throat.

I read an article recently on whether obesity can be labeled a "disease". I believe many factors can contribute to a person's weight, but at the end of the day no one dies of obesity. Take that how you will.

100. My First Full Arrest

There was a long period of time between my 99th partner and my 100th. Nearly a month went by with the same partners. I had a request from someone wanting to be my hundredth partner, because by that time I knew I would be writing this book and they wanted their story told. However this was not to be the case.

Slate and I had been going out together as partners every night we worked. We were a team. Made t-shirts and everything (no, seriously)! So when our supervisor asked or rather informed us that he needed coverage in one of the 911 districts we resisted. We liked working our little part in the big bad City. Sure it wasn't "real" EMS, but it was comfortable and none too traumatizing.

This time we were given no other choice, so we at least managed to stay together. We were sent out to this tiny town. Not quite as tiny as the one I worked at the fire station in Chapter 99, but not exactly a happening place.

Slate and I weren't enthusiastic, but we did our job and had only done one transfer run out of the local hospital. We were both exhausted, sleep deprived and eager to go home.

I sat in the driver's seat writing the first few chapters of this very book and watched the minutes tick by. Another unit was sent for fuel and we were sent to cover their town. Slate was passed out and we were only 15 minutes away from being able to call for fuel, when I heard the tones.

It was my sincerest hope that this run might fall on another town, another truck, but no, it was our run, our town. Then in the split second before the chief complaint was issued I prayed for something easy like a fall or a shortness of air or even a chest pain.

But then the mack daddy of chief complaints, the dreaded phrase was uttered, "Patient is unconscious, unresponsive. CPR is in progress."

Neither Slate nor I had worked a full arrest before. Neither of us had even performed CPR on anything but a dummy. I worked on getting the lights and sirens going while Slate got the address of the nursing home in the GPS.

When he said he couldn't find it in the GPS I grew frustrated. We needed to be there now! But then I saw my partner's hands shaking and I realized we needed to calm down and think.

Dispatch sent a paramedic intercept car, but he was coming from farther away. We got the address in and flew to the facility where our patient was. Even though I was freaking out on the inside and my mouth had gotten Sahara dry, I did my best to seem cool and collected.

I ran through what equipment we would need. I threw the backboard on the stretcher, Slate grabbed the AED and I made sure the BLS bag was there. It had nasal airways, oxygen masks, and a bag we might use.

We rushed in and the sight was reminiscent of an operating room. A group of people all dressed in blue gowns were clustered around a large woman on a bed. It was then I saw the big guy pushing down on her chest and a woman bagging the patient. I saw their AED attached and did some quick thinking.

I decided since nearly everything that we could do was being done for the patient, that the next step was getting her on our stretcher. I quickly undid every single strap in what seemed to be a forever and a half. As I got the stretcher into place, my vision fell to her limp arm, falling off the bed, the pale color of her skin, her blue tinted lips.

We moved her and it was then that I met my hundredth partner, paramedic Watson. He seemed gruff and asked if either of us was ALS. It seemed like a stupid question to me. If we were we wouldn't need you. My opinions stayed my own as I clambered to follow his orders. With Slate's help he got his monitor attached. The measured heart rhythm was asystole, or none. Shocking was not indicated. You can't shock a heart into beating again. You can only shock a confused heart into a better, more stable rhythm. Real life is not like the TV gentle readers.

This was not a best case scenario. With the knowledge that her heart was in asystole, I attempted to prepare myself for the worst. The medic got his ET, endotracheal, tube ready to intubate. He looked down her throat and paused, "Wait," he said, "Hold up!"

Everyone stopped. The entire room quieted. The silence was overwhelming, the tension in the air suffocating. I instantly realized what the medic saw, something's in her airway! The medic took a tool and extracted a partial denture from the back of her throat.

"How far was that down?" a voice asked.

"Pretty far down," the medic answered.

I felt the stream of unspoken questions run through the nurses and CNAs around me. 'Did we cause this? How did we miss that?'

While they were pondering my medic had got his ET tube in and he tried to bag her. Said she's "goosed" and suddenly the stillness was broken and we're racing again. I'm trying to grab our stuff, but the medic is yelling at me to leave it and the crappy AED is coming apart in my hands.

A nurse is doing CPR as best she can while navigating through doorways. The medic told Slate to jump on the stretcher and do CPR, but almost immediately he told him to get off. We somehow got this woman and all the equipment in our truck. Slate jumps in the back and I quickly secure the medic's intercept car, being sure to take the key with me and not lock it in the car.

I rush to the driver's seat and get everything set up. The closest hospital is ten minutes away, but I plan on halving that. I know I can't go too fast, but I definitely go twenty over on the highway. I try to play it cool still, but when I fumble over my medic's name on the radio, I know I'm not doing the best job of it. I do my very best to give the quickest, smoothest ride I could.

I hear vomiting in the back and I thought I heard breathing. A wicked hope bloomed within me. I only slowed down to prevent too sharp turns and finally for when my medic told me to smooth it out as he placed an IV.

It was the early morning hours of a Sunday, so traffic was thankfully close to non-existent. All I had to really concentrate on was not missing my turns, not throwing my medic and partner around and not getting all of us killed.

We got to the ER and there were two nurses waiting outside. I wanted more than two! I wanted the whole cast of Grey's Anatomy out there! Where were my team of ten doctors and nurses!? I parked and quickly headed out to help Slate and my medic.

Together Slate and I unloaded our patient, who was just shy of three hundred pounds, out of the truck. I got my chance to do CPR. It's painfully hard to do on a moving stretcher with a patient too large for its boundaries. We took the stretcher in and into the ER's resuscitation room. We transferred her over and got her disconnected as our medic gave report to the sole doctor in the room.

I got the stretcher out and breathed a sigh of relief. Our jobs were done. I looked over at Slate who shakily quickly excused himself to go to the bathroom. I tried to ease myself back into reality by cleaning the stretcher and fetching the medic various papers.

Once my partner came back from the bathroom I sought to get him out of the ER where they were still working our patient, so I suggested he go clean the back of the truck. I methodically cleaned the stretcher and watched them work the woman. I heard them talk about Epi and IVs.

I kept my post outside the code room except for when I was sent to fetch things. I wanted them to save her. I wanted all our hard work to mean something. I didn't want to lose my first patient. Then as I watched them work her, I lowered my expectations. Just a beat of the heart, a rhythm. A single light of hope. Just a speck.

But then they stopped. I wanted to scream, to yell "Don't give up! You can't!"

I've known death is inevitable for a very long time, but never before had I been so directly responsible for someone's life, and lost them to death. I watched them drape a white sheet over her, the body, and watched as a nurse got a toe tag. In life we adorn our necks, wrists, and fingers, but in death it is a single toe we adorn.

We finally got introduced properly to our medic, Watson. He tried to highlight the positives in our actions. For our first full arrest we did well, he said. Everyone's first full arrest is mess, he said. I tried to play it calm and collected, always, because now that

Watson didn't have a patient he was congenial and extremely collected, and perfectly unfazed that someone just died.

I'm calm, because that's what seasoned EMTs are after a bad call. Professional to the core. I could tell my partner was still shaken. He's not as good at hiding his feelings as I am. I had an entire childhood and adolescence of pretending to be okay with something's that not. He lacked my formal education in the matter.

Slate had said for a while that he would like to work a full arrest, so I asked him how he felt. He said he wasn't prepared for that. He didn't expect it to be like that. I agreed.

All I wanted to do after that run was leave, but we ended up spending an hour at the hospital, because our medic had to do his paperwork.

When we were finally free of Watson and that run, I felt the knowledge fall over me. I had lost my patient, my first patient. I needed a shot of liquor and some church.

I knew this moment would come eventually. I want to be a doctor. It was going to happen, not if, but when. I just wanted it to happen later, much later.

In the course of just a half hour, a person went from someone living to something unloving, something irreparably dead. In just thirty minutes she went from being a person to being like one of the bodies from a gross anatomy class I took in grad school.

I knew "the story". She was a 71 year old white female with congestive heart failure, acute renal failure, a previous myocardial infarction, and other chronic diseases. I knew she was obese. I knew her blood glucose level was only 30. I knew she was just admitted to the nursing home a week ago from the hospital. I knew that she was complaining of nausea before she was found unconscious.

I knew all this, but not a single thing about the type of person she was, who she was. Did she have anyone she loved? Who loved her? That should matter, right? Afterwards, all these EMTs were congratulating me on my first full arrest. I had gone through the baptismal font of EMS and finally earned the title of EMT. I was a "real" EMT. And I felt awful.

When I got home I did pour a shot of rum and raised my glass to the woman. I swiped at the tears forming in my eyes. The alcohol burned wonderfully on the way down and left me gasping. I limited myself to one shot, took a shower, and got ready for church.

I hadn't been to church in six months, but I knew I had to do this, not for myself, but for her. At church I still felt unclean, sitting amongst the bright, happy faces of well dressed families. Death was on my hands. I isolated myself by scribbling notes on my bulletin and I refused to look at anyone. I didn't want to infect them with what was weighing on my soul.

During the church service they said suffering is good. My EMS career had hardened my heart, but I couldn't, wouldn't blow this off. I embraced the hurt, because it meant despite Ryder, that at least I still cared. I had worried that my compassion had been destroyed by the pill poppers, abusers, and exposure to daily human suffering. I guess it hadn't, maybe lessened, but not destroyed.

Because, and I don't mean to be a God person – everyone has that thing which brings them solace. For me it's God. He kept me "relatively" sane, my kindness intact, and kept hope in my life. I did not know what meaning could be attributed to this death, but I had to hope that there was some reason.

It's too hard not to believe. It's too easy to be the cynic, the cold, rude EMS worker you see at City EMS. I didn't want to be like that. I don't want to be like that.

I strongly dislike leaving you, my gentle readers, on a somber note, so read on for one more chapter, my own.

101. The Author

I am not a great person. Surely by the time you reach this final chapter you have realized this simple fact. I mean who am I to judge some of my coworkers and patients so harshly? I don't think it's very fair of me to make fun of them without applying some of the same treatment to myself. So here goes:

I am a neat freak, a bossy, must-be-in-control woman with a bad temper. I am a know-it-all and when it comes to my accomplishments incredibly immodest. I'm two faced and far too critical of not just my coworkers, but everyone in my life. I don't respond well to criticism and yet I can find everyone else's mistakes.

In summation I am just as bad (if not differently bad) as those other people I criticize, but like with all my partners all these flaws make me human. There is no such thing as a perfect person if you dig deeply enough. It's all in how or even whether you hide those flaws.

My flaws are what help me to relate and find common ground with nearly every partner I have ever worked with. We're all fucked up in our own ways, straining to find meaning in this all too cruel world.

I hope to find my meaning in becoming a doctor and in telling the stories of the people in my life whether they like it or not! I hope in my tiny way I can bring healing to the world through medicine and through the words I write.

In the time since I first began to write the stories of my coworkers, I have applied to medical school and have been accepted. Truly I am about to start a new chapter in my life as I approach my quitting date at Ryder EMS and my starting date for med school. I have been at this company for three very long years, and while I am reluctant to say anything nice about it, I will say I will miss the people.

Since I started this book and had my hundredth partner, I have had about twenty more. They all remind me of the diversity of human personality that exists and the tapestry of genetics, experience and memory that is every human being. I can't say I liked everyone I worked with, in fact far from it. But even if I didn't like working with them, they sure made for a good story or two.

Thank you, gentle readers, for reading this monstrosity. I hope I at least managed to keep your attention for a few minutes and distract you from your daily toils.

About E.S.T.

E.S.T. works as an Emergency Medical Technician in The City. Her EMS company, Ryder EMS, is a for-profit (mostly) transfer ambulance service. E.S.T.'s hobbies include not being at work, attempting to get into medical school, and writing this book about her first hundred ambulance partners at Ryder EMS. Who would have time for anything else!?! If it wasn't obvious, this is E.S.T.'s first publication though she looks forward to inflicting her future creative pursuits on the world.

http://chuckinggranny.blogspot.com/

Made in United States
Orlando, FL
02 January 2022

12818993R00100